🗍🗍🗍🗍🗍🗍

A STRONG LAND & A STURDY

🗍🗍🗍🗍🗍🗍

A STRONG LAND
& A STURDY

🐚🐚🐚🐚🐚🐚

ENGLAND IN THE MIDDLE AGES

🐚🐚🐚🐚🐚🐚

Richard Barber

A CLARION BOOK

The Seabury Press · New York

The Seabury Press, 815 Second Avenue, New York, N.Y. 10017

Text copyright © 1976 by Richard Barber

First American Edition 1976

Library of Congress Cataloging in Publication Data

Barber, Richard W.
  A strong land and a sturdy: England in the Middle Ages.

"A Clarion book."
Bibliography
Includes index.
SUMMARY. Through a study of the political and social institutions, the rulers, artists, scientists and craftsmen of the Middle Ages, the author examines what everyday life in medieval times was like and what links with the era still survive.
  1. England—Social life and customs—Medieval period, 1066–1485—Juvenile literature. [1. England—Social life and customs—Medieval period, 1066–1485. 2. Civilization, Medieval] I. Title.
DA185.B23   942   75–43895
ISBN 0–8164–3167–1

Printed in Great Britain

ロロロロロ

CONTENTS

ロロロロロ

☖☖☖☖☖☖

ACKNOWLEDGEMENTS

☖☖☖☖☖☖

Acknowledgements are due to the following for permission to reproduce the colour and black and white plates:

Bodleian Library, Oxford, 5 (MS Jones 46 f. 50), 9 and 10 (MS Douce 180 f. 24 & 58), 11 (MS Ashmole 1523 f. 99), 12 (MS Ashmole 1511 f. 86v), 3 (MS Bodley 264 f. 72v), 5 (MS Bodley 581 f. 18v), 6 (MS Douce 158 f. 45), 12 (MS Rawl. D. 1220 f. 32), 13 (MS Selden Supra 38 f. 27), 15 (MS Gough Liturg. 7 f. 11), 29 (MS Douce 104 f. 46), 30 (MS Auct. D. 2.2. f. 133^v), 32 (MS Bodley 581 f. 24v), 55 (MS Douce 104 f. 33^b); British Tourist Authority, 40–43; Trustees of the British Library, 1 (MS Roy. 2. A.XXII f. 219), 16 (MS Cotton Aug. V f. 103), 19 (MS Roy. 17 E. III f. 36), 22 (MS Roy. 2. A.XXII f. 221), 23 (MS Harl. 5102 f. 37), 24 (MS Add. 28962 f. 281^v), 31 (MS Harl. 1585 f. 9^v), 36 (MS Cotton Nero. D. I f. 23^v), 47 (MS Roy. 14 C. VIII f. 90), 49 (MS Roy. 14 C. VIII f. 90^v), 50 (MS Add. 42130 f. 206^v), 54 (MS Arundel 91 f. 218^v), 56 (MS Cotton Claud. D. VI f. 12^v), 59 (MS Cotton Nero. D. I f. 3), 60 (MS Roy. 10 E.IV f. 65^v), 61 (MS Roy. 19 B. XV f. 37), 62 (MS Roy. 2 A. XXII f. 220); Trustees of the British Museum, 11, 63; Master and Fellows of Corpus Christi College, Cambridge, 1 (MS 61 f. 1^v), 48 (MS 16 f. 1^v); Master and Fellows of Corpus Christi College, Oxford, 2 (MS 161 f. 172), 7 (MS 285); A. F. Kersting, 6, 8, 25; Museum of the History of Science, Oxford, 33; National Gallery, 2, 3; National Maritime Museum, 57; National Monuments Record, 4, 8, 9, 10, 14, 17, 26, 28, 35, 39, 44, 52; Warden and Fellows of New College, Oxford, 18 (MS 288 f. 32); Pierpont Morgan Library, New York, 51 (MS 102 f. 2); Master and Fellows of Trinity College, Cambridge, 21 (MS R. 17. I); Earl of Verulam, 53; Trustees of the Victoria and Albert Museum, 45, 46; Woodmansterne Ltd, 4, 7, 27, 34, 37, 38, 58. The copyright in plate 20 is held by the author.

᳁᳁᳁᳁᳁᳁

THE COMING OF THE NORMANS

᳁᳁᳁᳁᳁᳁

'FROM the fury of the Northmen, good Lord deliver us!' This prayer echoed through many French churches about the year 900, as the Viking leader Rolf raided and plundered the rich farms and villages of Brittany and northern France. For once, however, the raiders did not merely gather their booty and return home. They were defeated by the army of Charles III in 911, and by 918 had become his subjects. They settled on the coast of what we now call Normandy, named after these Northmen or Normans.

A settled life and their conversion to Christianity did not change their restless ambition. Under Rolf's son, William Long-sword, they began to expand their territory. Within a hundred years the duchy over which Rolf's descendants ruled was one of the greatest provinces of France. When it suited them, the Vikings had no hesitation in going back to paganism, or seeking help from their pirate relations who still terrorized much of Europe. Even the first duke of Normandy seemed 'a pirate chief' to a Frenchman living a hundred miles away.

Before a century had passed, however, they were accepted by the French as part of the Kingdom of France, and their ambitions had turned elsewhere. The younger sons of the families who ruled Normandy began to look for new places where a strong arm and a shrewd head might earn them a lordship of their own. A Norman knight who arrived by chance in southern Italy in 1047 saw good opportunities there, and other knights went to join him. Though the Italians disliked them, they were unable to keep these bold adventurers out. An Italian wrote of them soon after they came:

> The Normans are a most cunning race, taking revenge for injuries in the hope of profiting from them, despising those who till the fields, eager for gains and power, deceiving in all things, wavering between generosity and meanness. Their princes enjoy the greatest of good reputations; they are a people who know how to flatter, and who devote themselves to the study of eloquence, so that you listen even to their boys as you might listen to trained speakers. Although they have to be compelled to obey the law, they are untroubled by hard work, hunger or cold, when these are inflicted on them; they are patient as well. They are devoted to hunting and hawking. They delight in splendid horses and other equipment of war, as well as in fine clothing.*

The Normans came to Italy by chance rather than design. England was a much more obvious target, even though the twenty miles of sea which separated it from Normandy was a frightening obstacle to the sailors of the eleventh century. The Danish King Canute, whose empire had included Denmark, England and parts of Sweden, was the last really strong ruler in England, and he had died in 1016. King Edward (called 'the Confessor' because of his holy life) had come to the throne in 1042, but he had no children. By the middle of the eleventh century, there were many Normans and Frenchmen at his court, because he liked their company. So it was not surprising that the Normans should be very interested in who was going to be the next king. Their duke, William, had a claim to the English throne himself, under the complicated and often vague rules about what happened when there were no direct heirs. When Edward died, William at once planned to cross the Channel with an army and try to make good this claim.

The story of Harold's brave resistance to both William's invasion and that of the Norwegians in the north has already been told by Kevin Crossley-Holland in *Green Blades Rising*.† William triumphed partly because Harold's men were exhausted

---

* Geoffrey Malaterra, *The Deeds of Roger Count of Sicily* I, 3 (author's translation).
   † Kevin Crossley-Holland: *Green Blades Rising*, The Seabury Press, New York, 1976.

by their long march south after their victory at Stamford, and partly because the Normans were fearsome and well-equipped warriors, with much experience of war: some of William's men had fought in Sicily and learned new tactics there. But only a leader with the bold and adventurous spirit of the Normans would have embarked on such an attempt in the first place.

What drove the Normans on to these great adventures? Ambition, for the most part; and also, a recurring theme throughout the next centuries, the need to provide for younger sons. A gradual change, difficult to trace exactly, had come over the way men's goods were divided among their heirs. Where once all the sons had an equal claim, it was now agreed that the father's lands and titles went to the eldest son. Otherwise a rich and powerful family would find its estates broken up in the space of twenty or thirty years: if a man's four sons each had four sons, there would be sixteen heirs to divide up his lands, and from being nobles they would soon be peasants. So the younger sons were made to seek their own fortunes. In later centuries, they would go into the church, or into royal service. But the fierce-blooded Normans preferred to live by the sword. Even their bishops, like Odo of Bayeux, were happier on horseback, war-club in hand, than on their knees in prayer. Younger sons, proud of their noble descent, were ambitious for lands as well as glory. So William's invasion of England was not merely brought about by his own personal claim to the throne and his own ambition.

What distinguished the Normans from the earlier Vikings was their desire for lands they could own and rule, not just booty to carry off. The Anglo-Saxons had been great warriors, but it took them centuries to work out a system of just and strong government. The Normans managed to be both brilliant fighters and superb administrators, able both to conquer and rule a country well. They showed this ability in Sicily as well as England, and even the defeated English admitted it:

This King William of whom we speak was a very wise man, and very powerful and more worshipful and stronger than any predecessor of his had been. He was gentle to the good men who loved

God, and stern beyond measure to those people who resisted his will . . . Also he was very dignified . . . Amongst other things the good security he made in this country is not to be forgotten – so that any honest man could travel over his kingdom without injury with his pockets full of gold; and no man dared kill another.*

But their rule was not always just: the writer goes on: 'Certainly in his time there was much oppression . . . He was sunk in greed and utterly given up to avarice . . .' This, too, was typical of the Normans. The Anglo-Saxons had valued freedom, and their kings had taxed them lightly, except when the Danes exacted the ransom called 'danegeld'. The Normans preferred to make the most of their new possessions. At the end of William's reign, he ordered a detailed survey of England to be made. Because it was so like the great reckoning up of affairs which the church had taught men to expect on the Day of Judgement, the book in which the results were recorded was called 'Doomsday Book'. It is an astonishing piece of work, in its detail and organization. Since Roman times, no one had ever tried to survey more than a single estate. One writer says about it 'There went out a decree from the King, that all England should be taxed', clearly echoing the Bible's words 'There went out a decree from Caesar Augustus, that all the world should be taxed'. 'Doomsday' gives minute details of almost the whole of England:

In the twentieth year of his reign, by order of William, King of the English, there was made a survey of the whole of England, that is to say of the lands of the several provinces of England and of the possessions of each and all of the magnates. This was done in respect of ploughlands and habitations, and of men both bond and free, both those who dwelt in cottages, and those who had their homes and their share in the fields; and in respect of ploughs and horses and other animals: and in respect of the services and payments due from all men in the whole land. Other investigators followed the first; and men were sent into provinces which they did not know, and where they were themselves unknown, so they might be given the chance

* Anglo-Saxon Chronicle, entry for the year 1086.

to check the first survey, and if need be, denounce the authors of it as guilty to the King. And the land was troubled with much violence because of the collection of the royal taxes.*

Everything was recorded three times:

as it was in the time of King Edward; as it was when King William gave the estate; and as it is now. And it was also noted whether more could be taken from the estate than is now being taken.

Sometimes the entry reminds us vividly that this was a conquered land, uneasy under the Norman rule. Firstly, almost all the lords are Norman: the whole of the old Anglo-Saxon ruling class was destroyed or dispossessed. Secondly, the northern counties had threatened to rebel in the years immediately after 1066, and William had brutally laid waste great areas from Yorkshire northwards to the border with the independent kingdom of Scotland. The scars of the 'harrying of the North' showed in the Doomsday survey, where the bare entry 'Laid waste' occurs again and again, and the lands had scarcely recovered a century later.

The Normans were ruthless, ambitious, doing nothing by half-measures but always completely committed to what they undertook. The Norman state in England often seems like a dim forerunner of modern dictatorships, efficient and impersonal. So indeed it was; but England had lacked strong government for too long, and if the government had been weak, freedom and justice would have made even less progress. Without the Normans, England would have remained an unimportant island on the fringes of the Christian world, looking to Scandinavia rather than Europe. The Normans not only made it a highly organized state, but they also made England part of Europe again. Since Roman days, there had been no definite connection between England and the Continent. The Anglo-Saxons had been more concerned with what was happening in Scandinavia and with the Danish empire there. Now that the King of England was also

---

* Robert de Losinga, Bishop of Hereford: quoted in D. C. Douglas: *William the Conqueror*. London, 1966, pp. 348–9.

Duke of Normandy, England began to play an important role in European politics.

Almost the only contact with Europe, in Anglo-Saxon times, had been through churchmen. This was because of the links between the English church and the pope in Rome. He was recognized as the ruler of all Christians, and special cases and new laws meant that the English bishops were always in touch with Rome. As the church became more and more organized, these contacts with Europe grew more frequent. Indeed, by the fourteenth century many people began to complain that the English church was too Roman and European. They said it was out of touch with ordinary folk, full of Italians and foreign preachers, and that the Pope was taking away England's wealth through the riches which the church had accumulated.

In the centuries after the Norman conquest, many other contacts with Europe developed. Merchants, who had crossed the Channel only on rare occasions in the twelfth century, now made regular journeys. The great trade routes had begun to appear: wine came from Bordeaux, wool went to the weavers of Holland and Belgium, corn came from north Germany. Certain towns became famous for special skills: steel blades from Toledo in Spain, armour from Milan, enamelled jewellery from Limoges in France. Men travelled not only for worldly gain, but for the good of their minds and souls. Paris and Bologna were the first great universities of Europe and, until Oxford was founded about 1160, Paris was the nearest place where an English student could get more than a basic education. Pilgrims set out from England to worship at Rome, at the great shrine of St James at Santiago de Compostela in north-west Spain, or at Jerusalem itself. Until 1204 (when Normandy was conquered by the French king) the English king's messengers and the king himself moved restlessly backwards and forwards across the English Channel. After 1204, there were still royal links between England and Gascony, the English lands in south-west France, which lasted until the 1450s. Diplomacy, the art of settling political differences peacefully, was becoming much more important. For example, in one very busy month in November 1176, there came to Henry II's court at

Westminster separate embassies from the emperor of Byzantium at Constantinople; from Frederick Barbarossa, emperor of Germany; from Henry, duke of Saxony; from the archbishop of Rheims; from the count of Flanders; and from two of the Spanish kingdoms, Castile and Navarre.

The twelfth century was a marvellously rich period in Europe in many ways, as government became more organized, and people enjoyed a peace that had been unknown for centuries. The great cathedrals were built, the universities appeared, and huge progress was made in learning, literature and thought. It was also the beginning of a less happy development. The idea of 'nations' was almost unknown in the eleventh century; people thought of themselves as part of the Christian world, though they and their neighbours might be ruled by different princes. Latin was the common language for official business and for the church. Literature in the twelfth century was mostly in Latin. The first great version of the story of King Arthur was written in Latin by a Welshman. But increasingly the languages of the ordinary people, Saxon, French, German or Spanish, came to be used for state affairs and for everything except ceremonial and religious occasions. When Spanish ambassadors came to London in 1176, the speeches had to be written down because the English could not understand Latin spoken with a Spanish accent. By the fourteenth century, Latin was no longer a common spoken language.

French had been the court language since Norman days and provided an easy way of continuing links with Europe. When, in the middle of the thirteenth century popular literature started to be written in the different everyday languages, Englishmen wrote and read in French. Even in the fifteenth century French romances were still popular in England. English was slower to develop because of this continuing use and knowledge of French. It was only with the poetry of Chaucer, at the end of the fourteenth century, that English literature, blending both Norman and Anglo-Saxon traditions, came into its own. At Richard II's court a European visitor would have found one or two people who spoke only English.

With this change of language came a change in attitudes towards other people. At the same time, as languages became more distinct, so people began to think of themselves as members of nations. Once it was a question of 'Who is your lord?' The king of England was lord of English and Norman alike, though he held Normandy from the king of France. But gradually it became a question of homeland or nation, and which king was less important than which kingdom: instead of being the 'king of England's man', you were an Englishman, speaking English and regarding Frenchmen as strangers; while the French claimed to believe that Englishmen had tails! At first, only ordinary people, who did not travel very much, believed this kind of thing. (Many humble folk never went more than a mile or two from the village where they were born.) But gradually the great lords and merchants as well came to regard foreigners as something different. This was because of the change in language and the new idea of nations, and it only came about at the very end of the Middle Ages.

Reading the pages of Jean Froissart's chronicles in the fourteenth century, it is the common factor of chivalry and knighthood that matters, not the differences of French and English. Who wins a battle, in Froissart's view, is less interesting than the great deeds done in the course of the fighting. Froissart himself says as much:

> That the honourable enterprises, noble adventures, and deeds of arms, performed in the wars between England and France, may be properly related, and held in perpetual remembrance – to the end that brave men taking example from them may be encouraged in their well-doing I sit down to record a history deserving great praise.

At the same period, the knight in Chaucer's *Canterbury Tales* thought of knighthood as something that was above being patriotic and supporting just one nation: he had fought for Christendom at Alexandria in Egypt, in Prussia, in Spain and Morocco, with the crusading armies who were trying to conquer heathen lands.

The church and knighthood both helped to unite Europe in

the Middle Ages. The two came together in the crusades.★ These expeditions aimed to recover and keep the Holy City, Jerusalem, for Christendom which had fallen into the hands of the Moslems. The first crusade, in 1099, succeeded against all the odds in capturing Jerusalem; but there were immense difficulties in holding a fortress so far from the nearest friendly land. So new armies set out at intervals, whenever Jerusalem was threatened by the Moslems from whom it had been captured. These armies were drawn from the whole of Europe. At first rich and poor alike set out, but only the properly organized armies made the journey successfully, and the enthusiastic crowds of poor people were massacred on the way by brigands. By the time Richard the Lionheart went on crusade, a hundred years after the first crusade, the crusading armies were divided along national lines, and quarrels between French, English and Germans prevented the expedition from being a success. But the crusade remained one of the ideals of all European knights; and the leaders of the church tried to use it to stop the kings of Europe from fighting among themselves by calling on them to unite and save Christendom from the attacks of the pagans. For although there might be rival claimants for the pope's throne, all Christian men thought of themselves as part of a single world, of which England was an important part.

★ See p. 117 below.

🔁🔁🔁🔁🔁

THE KING AND HIS COURT

🔁🔁🔁🔁🔁

WALTER MAP was one of the courtiers of Henry II, and he gives a lively description of the king and his court in his book *Courtiers' Tales*, written about 1185:

> King Henry was rather above average height, straight-limbed and with an attractive face, the kind of man whom people would run to see again even if they had already seen him a thousand times. He was second to none in physical activity, as adventurous as anyone else, as courteous and skilled in arms as a nobleman should be, well-educated and able to hold his own in any conversation, both social and about business, because he knew all the languages spoken from the Atlantic coast to Palestine (though he only used Latin and French). When it came to making laws or reforming the government he was shrewd and clever at discovering new and secret ways of doing justice; he was easily approached, polite and not proud; he put up with bad conditions on the road; he was often ill and often harmed, but he did not complain. He travelled endlessly, and rode for long stretches like a messenger, not thinking about the people who had to ride with him. He was a good judge of hounds and falcons, and very fond of hunting. He could go for nights without sleep, and never tired of action.

Henry II was an exceptional king; but even under less outstanding rulers the court was the centre of the kingdom. All matters of government, law and finance were settled there; and it was also the place where poets and musicians looked for their audience. The great nobles gathered there both for business

1. A king, drawn by Matthew Paris in the early 13th century.

and for pleasure. But although the king had his great palaces at Westminster and elsewhere, the court was not at a fixed place: it was wherever the king happened to be. Peter of Blois, who was often at Henry's court, has left this description of what could happen when the king was on his travels:

If the king has promised to remain in a place for that day – and especially when he has announced his intention publicly by the mouth of a herald – he is sure to upset all the arrangements by departing early in the morning. As a result, you see men dashing around as if they were mad, beating their pack-horses, running their carts into one another – in short, giving a lively imitation of Hell. If, on the other hand, the king orders an early start, he is certain to change his mind, and you can take it for granted that he will sleep until mid-day. Then you will see the packhorses loaded and waiting, the carts prepared, the courtiers dozing, traders fretting, and everyone grumbling . . . When our courtiers had gone ahead almost the whole day's ride, the king would turn aside to some other place where he had, it might be, just a single house with accommodation for himself and no one else. I hardly dare say it, but I believe that in truth he took a delight in seeing what a fix he put us in. After wandering some three or four miles in an unknown wood, and often in the dark, we thought ourselves lucky if we stumbled upon some filthy little hovel. There was often a sharp and bitter argument about a mere hut, and swords were drawn for possession of a lodging that pigs would have shunned.

By the end of the fourteenth century the court had become a much more complicated body. Parts of it had become the great law courts and the treasury, most of whose work was done at the Exchequer in Westminster. The Chancery, which saw that the king's orders were carried out, was also settled there. And the king himself was no longer so ready to travel round the country. Edward III had been a warrior-king, and his court had been made up of soldiers. Its favourite occupations were war and tournaments, and the Order of the Garter was founded by Edward to reward great prowess in both of these. The court was the centre of good manners and polished behaviour, and 'courtly' came to mean these things. Under Richard II, Edward's successor, the court became something new, a brilliant pageant in which the king was the star. For a brief period, the English court was the most dazzling in Europe, where new fashions and new ideas were eagerly explored. Learning and the arts were valued more than feats of arms. Richard himself read romances in French and English, and liked to buy richly decorated and bound manuscripts; and he asked great poets to write works for him. One of the loveliest miniatures of the period shows Geoffrey Chaucer reading his works to a courtly audience (see colour plate 1). The first individual style in English painting appears in his reign: there is a famous portrait of the king with his three patron saints (perhaps portraits of his father, the Black Prince, and grandfather, Edward III) which forms part of the altarpiece called the Wilton Diptych* (see colour plate 2). Richard's personal badge, the white hart, appears not only on the back of the altarpiece (see colour plate 3), but is also worn by the angels of the court of heaven. In the minds of medieval men, kings were next only to God; and Richard's splendid dress and splendid palaces were designed to underline the difference between him and other men. Once he is said to have sat on his throne all afternoon, without speaking, and when he looked at any of the courtiers standing round him, the man he looked at had to kneel to him.

Just as the king attached great importance to outward splendour, so his courtiers followed. Richard himself is reputed to have had a suit which cost more than £1000, while his courtiers wore extravagantly wide sleeves that almost touched the ground (see plate 2), and like the king, used little squares of linen called handkerchiefs instead of wiping their noses on these sleeves. The ordinary people did not have much time for such extravagance, and satires on the fashionable lords were common:

> You proud gallants heartless
> With your high caps witless
> And your short gowns thriftless
> With your long peaked shoes
> (For them your purse is almost empty)
> Have brought this land to great pain.

Nonetheless Richard lived in an age of peace and relative plenty. For the first time since Roman days, the nobles no longer

---

* A painting made of two panels hinged together.

2. Early 15th century costume in the style
worn by Richard II's courtiers.

had to concentrate entirely on defending their lands and feeding
their followers, and men were ready to spend their riches rather
than hoarding them in chests or burying them in the ground. So
rich garments and displays of wealth were part of court life in
peacetime. This new-found way of impressing your friends could
reach absurd heights, though the best examples are not from
England. At a feast in southern France in 1177, all the food was
cooked over wax candles, while in Siena in the thirteenth century,
a group of rich young men called the 'Spendthrift Brigade' used
to have gold coins cooked in a sauce; they then sucked the sauce
off the coins and threw them away. Neither Richard's court, nor

3. A court feast, from a Flemish manuscript of about 1340.

any other English court in the Middle Ages, reached quite these extravagances.

Besides fine clothes, Richard and his courtiers also loved fine food and lovely houses. Richard's cooks were always preparing new and strange dishes for him, and the cookery book which they compiled influenced what noble households ate for the next three centuries (see plate 3). Richard's palaces, too, were splendid; they were no longer castles, designed for defence, with heavy walls and small windows, but light, airy buildings decorated with wall-paintings and rich tiles. In his palace at Sheen there was even a bath with bronze taps for hot and cold water, a luxury unknown since Roman times. He and his beloved queen, Anne of Bohemia, spent much time at Sheen, and when she died, Richard ordered the palace to be rased to the ground, because he could not bear to go there without her. He rebuilt his other palaces in similar style: the work at Great Hall at Westminster was carried out for him by Henry Yevele (see p. 85).

In this glittering court moved two of the most outstanding poets that England produced in the Middle Ages: Geoffrey Chaucer and John Gower. Gower was a man of independent means, but Chaucer was both poet and royal official. In Saxon and Norman days, a man with a gift for learning and literature had only one career open to him: the church. But now, under the Plantagenet kings, the royal household offered a new way for clever men; and for someone like Chaucer whose interests had little in common with the closed world of the church. He began his career in 1357 as a page in the household of Edward III's daughter-in-law, Elizabeth, at the age of about thirteen, and with the exception of a seven year gap when he may have studied law, he remained with the court until his death in 1400. It is possible that many of his offices were given to him as a reward for his poems. When he was made head of the London customs, he was soon given leave to appoint someone else to do the work. Both in the church and royal service, the man appointed to an office was simply responsible for seeing that the work was done. If he could find someone else to do it for less than he was paid, this was quite all right. On the other hand, this system did not work so well with important jobs. When Chaucer was appointed clerk of the works, in charge of all the king's buildings, he seems to have found it too much, because although he appointed a deputy, he only held the office for two years, from 1389 to 1391. After that he relied on the king's goodwill for his living; and Richard was a generous patron, giving him a pension and lending him money as he needed it.

Chaucer is typical of the courtiers of Richard's reign, interested first and foremost in the court's amusements and diversions, its

4. William of Wykeham's effigy on his tomb in Winchester Cathedral.

poetry, art and good living. But the royal service was also a high-road for clever men with ambition. Under Edward III, one of these was William of Wykeham, Lord Chancellor of England, of whom Froissart once wrote 'a priest called Sir William de Wican reigned in England . . . by him everything was done and without him they did nothing'. (See plate 4.) He had started as the son of a freeman, and after a good education, became assistant to the sheriff of Hampshire. In his early twenties he started work in the royal service. Within five years he was clerk of the works at Windsor Castle, and one of the towers there bears the inscription 'This made Wykeham', meaning both that Wykeham built it, and that it made Wykeham's fortune. The inscription, though Wykeham did not put it there himself, was true enough: after another eight years he was one of the most important officers in the kingdom, and remained one of the king's right-hand men until his death in 1400. But even so powerful a man depended on the king's favour: in 1376, Wykeham took part in the trial of Alice Perrers, Edward III's mistress. Alice Perrers regained the king's favour later that year, and in 1377 it was Wykeham's turn to be tried and disgraced as a result of her schemes against him. The disgrace did not last long, for Edward III died in June, and Richard II soon pardoned him. The rewards of a courtier might be great (Wykeham left a huge fortune), but the risks were

5. The executioner,
from a late 14th century manuscript.

great, too, when the king was unable to protect his servants or favourites:

> The axe was sharp, the block was hard
> In the fourteenth year of King Richard. (See plate 5)

Much of both Chaucer's and Gower's poetry is overshadowed by the dark image of the 'Wheel of Fortune': a man's life is seen as a great wheel on which he sits in a chair. He rises slowly to the highest point, the chair overturns as it begins to descend, and he falls headlong (see plate 6). Richard himself, lord of this rich court, was hurled from Fortune's Wheel in 1399, when Henry Bolingbroke deposed him and had him put to death.

6. The wheel of fortune.

A NOBLEMAN AND HIS HOUSEHOLD

MEDIEVAL men attached great importance to correct behaviour and to elaborate ritual. The motto of Winchester College, founded in the fourteenth century, was 'Manners make the man', and anyone who hoped to make a good career, particularly at court, was expected to know how to behave and what the correct procedure was on any occasion. Most sons of nobles were given a suitable training, by being sent to live in a great household, usually with another family than their own. For just as the king had his court and courtiers, so the noblemen who ruled great areas of England had their own courts. Some of these families became very powerful. The Bigods, Bohuns, de la Poles or Percys were like independent princes. They were often able to defy the king himself, though the king usually won in the end. Like the king, they would often take their household with them as they moved round the country. It would be organized like a miniature court, with its own exchequer and law officers, who were allowed to deal with 'low' justice or minor offences which happened on the lord's lands (see pp. 30–33). By the fifteenth century, however, the household was usually settled at the lord's main home; and it had become less powerful as the king's control over local affairs increased.

This change was reflected in the kind of house in which the great lords lived. In the first years after the Normans came to England, they built castles of wood, throwing up earth mounds if there was no suitable natural site that could be defended. These protected them against a surprise attack by the Saxons, who remained a possible danger until about 1100. As soon as they were sufficiently well organized, the Normans replaced these wooden castles with stone ones, which involved much more skill and effort to build. In troubled times such as those of the civil war between King Stephen and his rival Matilda, these were a safe refuge, while the poor folk outside the castle walls suffered, as the Anglo-Saxon Chronicle for 1137 says in one of its last entries:

> For every powerful man built his castles . . . and they filled the country full of castles. When the castles were built, they filled them with devils and wicked men. Then, both by night and day, they took those people that they thought had any goods – and . . . tortured them with indescribable tortures to extort gold and silver. They were hung by the thumbs or by the head, and heavy armour was hung on their feet. Knotted ropes were put round their heads and twisted until they penetrated to the brains. They put them in prisons where there were adders and snakes and toads, and killed them like that.

One of Henry II's first actions on becoming king was to destroy many of these newly built castles; and after that a castle could only be built by buying from the king, usually for a high price, a 'licence to crenellate', that is, to put up fortifications. As warfare grew less and less frequent in England, so the nobles began to build unfortified houses, copying the new palaces which the kings were building, which were no longer the prison-like, thick-walled fortresses, but lighter and airier and more pleasant to live in. It was in a house such as this, or in a castle converted to the new style, that the squire described by Chaucer in the *Canterbury Tales* learned how to behave and how to make his mark in the fashionable world:

> Singing he was, or fluting, all the day,
> He was as fresh as is the month of May.
> Short was his gown, with sleeves long and wide.
> Well could he sit on horse, and fairly ride.
> He could make songs, and sing them well,

Joust, and dance too, as well as draw and write.
He was so hot a lover that at night
He slept no more than does a nightingale.
Courteous he was, humble, and quick to serve,
And carved before his father at the table.

It might surprise us to find such a fine young man given the job of carving: but serving at table was regarded as a noble duty. Some of the great officers of the king's court had originally been men who served the king at table, and on state occasions they still did so. When in 1356 the Black Prince wished to honour the king of France, whom he had taken prisoner at the battle of Poitiers, he 'himself served at the king's table, with every mark of humility, and would not sit down at it, in spite of all the king's entreaties for him to do so'.

To the traveller, coming to such a place from his weary battle across the country tracks, the nobleman's house was a more than welcome refuge. Merchants and humbler folk were often allowed in, because there was still a tradition that a lord should keep open house, and writers complained about some lords who dined in private to avoid all the people in the hall. But anyone of equal rank would be an honoured guest, in an age when the guest was still regarded as someone special. In the fourteenth century romance *Sir Gawain and the Green Knight*, Gawain finds such a welcome after a journey through wild lands in wild weather:

At the chimneyed hearth where charcoal burned, a chair was placed
For Sir Gawain in gracious style, gorgeously decked
With cushions on quilted work, both cunningly wrought;
And then a magnificent mantle, maroon in hue,
Of the finest fabric, and fur-lined with ermine,
As was the hood, was elegantly laid on him;
Perfect were the pelts, the most precious on earth.
In that splendid seat he sat in dignity,
And warmth came to him at once, bringing well-being.*

* Sir Gawain and the Green Knight: translated by Brian Stone. Penguin, Harmondsworth, 1959.

៙៙៙៙៙៙

THE MANOR AND THE VILLAGE

៙៙៙៙៙៙

MOST people in England in the Middle Ages lived in the country. The map of the countryside has altered very little since those days, and almost all today's settlements – hamlets, villages or small towns – can be traced back to the beginning of the Middle Ages. Only where the great towns have expanded and swallowed up the surrounding country has the pattern changed very much, and even then old names and roads often survive under the crop of new buildings. Most village and town names can be traced back to this period, and they often refer to things that can still be seen today. The village where I am writing this has been called Alderton since at least 1086, and the alder trees still grow along the hedgerows.

But the medieval countryside would have looked very different. For one thing, there would have been few hedgerows: great open fields (not unlike those produced by modern farming methods) would have contrasted with even larger areas of woodland, heath and uncultivated land. The open fields would have been divided into strips, each marked off by a turf bank: these were the tiny individual plots of the villagers, and among these village holdings would be those of the lord of the manor.

For the 'village' was not really a self-contained unit, in the way that a town would be, with a single council to govern it. One village would have several manors around it, belonging to different lords: and the lord of the manor was the most important person in a villager's life. If the villager was a serf or villain, the lord actually owned him, like a piece of property, and he could not leave the village without his permission. He could be bought and sold, as could his children, who also belonged to the lord. If he was a freeman, he would still owe service to the lord; which meant usually that he had to do so many days' work for him, and pay certain taxes. And all minor arguments and lawsuits were settled by the lord's officials in the manor court. Life was hard for the villagers, whether free or serfs (see plate 7); and when a man reached the end of his working days, there were no pensions or security for him:

> Lyard is an old horse and cannot pull a cart:
> He shall be put out to grass with holly as his food
> Barefoot, without his shoes, there shall he go,
> For he is now an old horse, and may not work again.
> While that Lyard could pull, so then he was loved:
> They gave him provisions, and he provided work.
> Now he cannot do the work that he once used to do
> They give him plain pea-straw and take away the corn.
> They take him to the smithy to strike off his shoes
> And put him in the woodland, which shall be his home.
> Whoever cannot do his work, he must go to grass,
> Barefoot, without his shoes, and go with Lyard.*

The records of the manor court are among the very few documents which give us some idea of village life, though they are concerned only with the villagers' worries, problems and misdeeds. Take for instance Richard Bradwater's appearances in his lord's court. Richard was a tenant at Tooting Bec, now a London suburb, where he held 13 acres of land of his own on a rent of 12d, and looked after 9 acres of his nephew's land. He had a cottage and garden as well, and was one of the richest serfs on the manor, though also one of the most difficult. His first summons, in 1394, was a technical one, by which he was asked to show his copy of the deeds to his property. But several courts later in 1397, he still had not done so, and was now in trouble because his pigs had trespassed on the lord's meadow. He had

---

* Author's translation from the original in the Oxford Book of Medieval Verse. O.U.P. Oxford, 1967.

7. The labours of the months, from a manuscript of about 1280

A. January: the god Janus feasting   B. February: by the fireside

c. March: pruning trees   D. April: planting a tree

E. May: picking flowers   F. June: haymaking

G. July: reaping the corn

H. August: threshing
· (to separate out the grain)

I. September: treading
grapes to make wine

J. October: sowing

K. November: knocking down
acorns for pigs to eat

L. December: killing a pig
for the Christmas feast

1. Chaucer reading his works to a courtly audience

2. The Wilton Diptych:
Richard II worships the Virgin Mar[...]
The two patron saints beside h[...]
are portraits of Edward I[...]
and the Black Prin[...]

3. The Wilton Diptych:
Richard II's badge, the white hart

also beaten the lord's bailiff when he tried to collect the lord's taxes, and he had held two acres of land to which he was not entitled. Six months later it is his cattle which have strayed into his neighbour's crops; another year, and his cattle have been in his lord's grain, and he has mowed hay belonging to the lord and taken it away. In the autumn of 1399, there is for once some peaceful business, recording that he and his wife have taken over some cottages and land from a relative; but he is also in trouble for assaulting a neighbour and seizing a stray pig. The record goes on, always in this same vein: everything centres on the land and its cultivation, with only an occasional reference to other matters, and even then it is usually a matter of illicit brewing by the peasants (they were only allowed to buy beer at the lord's licensed alehouse).

Richard Bradwater's cottage would have been a simple building. Simplest of all was the cruck cottage, found mostly in the north and west, which consisted of two pairs of wooden pieces propped against each other to form a V upside down (see plate 8). A ridge-piece was then set on the point of each V, and the basic framework was ready for walling and thatching. Wattle and daub would be used for the walls, and the windows would be closed by wooden shutters. But Bradwater lived near London, and his cottage might have had a more elaborate box-frame, needing more skill in carpentry. Brick was a rarity until the sixteenth century; and as a result simple houses had no chimneys. In winter even the most hardened men must have found them uncomfortable, filled with smoke, draughty, often scarcely proof against the rain.

The lord himself was not all that much more comfortable. Many of the lesser lords were only a little better off than the freemen, and Richard Bradwater was almost as rich as a freeman. Such lords would not have had castles, but simply a larger version of the cottage. This, in the later Middle Ages, became the elaborate manor house (see plate 9). Early manors were simply a central hall with a separate room for sleeping and sometimes a smaller dining hall; in areas where stone was easily available, an extra storey was sometimes added. But by the fifteenth century the

8. Cruck cottage at Didbrook in Gloucestershire:
the frame is two large pieces of timber propped against each other.

manor house was an elaborate and often very lovely building. Very
few new castles were being built, and great lords now lived in
houses of this type (see plate 10). The central hall remained, but
there were more elaborate groups of rooms at each end, usually a
kitchen and stores to one end, and a solar and bedrooms at the

9. 12th century manor house at Boothby Pagnell, Lincolnshire, with the entrance on the upper floor.

10. 15th century manor house at Ockwells, Berkshire: an elaborate building with glazed windows.

other. The solar, meaning a sun-room, came from the Latin word
for the room where people sat and took their ease, and was used
by the family, while the hall was for formal occasions. Many
such houses survive, often much altered, with the hall divided
into two storeys or disguised behind a Georgian façade: but
occasionally an untouched example remains as a living illustration
of medieval life. Only the churches, to which we shall return,
offer a more direct contact with the period.

Unless the village was in one of the heavily populated parts of
England, there would be waste land, heath or forest, separating it
from the next settlement; and across much of England stretched
the forest, just as it had always been since man first knew it. But
this was far from being open to everyone: the forest was the most
jealously guarded area of all, for it was here that the king hunted
(see plate 11). From William I, 'who loved the stags as if he were

11. A hawking party, from a 14th century ivory.

their father', king after king had asserted the forest law to protect his favourite sport, until many areas which were quite heavily farmed came within the boundaries of the royal forests. The land in the forest might belong to anyone, but the forest hunting laws applied just the same. The New Forest, as its name implies, was created specially for hunting, and many men's lands deliberately turned into a wilderness. The forest laws were harsh, but none-theless the daring poacher took his chance, and often got away with it:

> In the month of May, when mirths are many,
> And the season of summer when soft is the weather,
> Then I went to the woods, to try my luck,
> Into the shrubs to seek for a shot
> At a hart or a hind, happen as it might:
> And as the Lord drove the day from the heaven,
> Then I stayed on a bank by the brook's side,
> Where the grass was green, growing with flowers –
> Primrose and periwinkle, rich pennyroyal.
> The dew on the daisies shone there and sparkled
> On bud and on blossom, on branches most sweetly,
> And the soft mists began to lift gently.
> The cuckoo and cushat both sang keenly,
> And throstles trilled cheerfully in the banks,
> And each bird in the wood was glad as the next
> That darkness was done and the day dawning.
> Harts and hinds go to the hillsides
> The fox and the polecat seek out their earths,
> The hare huddles by hedgerows, hurries hastily home,
> Finds fast her forme and makes ready to settle.
> As I stood in that place, I thought I'd try stalking;
> Both my body and my bow I covered with leaves;
> And turned towards a tree and tarried there awhile;
> And as I looked at a clearing quite close to me,
> I saw a hart with high antlers grown on his head . . .
> A feast fit for a king, whoever might catch him.* .

* *The Parlement of the Thre Ages*, author's translation.

The risks of being caught were great; but poaching was a welcome change from the cares of everyday life. Other men sought their escape in less profitable pleasures:

> Ye follow not your fathers that fostered you all
> A kind harvest to catch and corn to win,
> 'Gainst the cold winter and keen, with clinging frosts,
> And the dropless drought in the dead months after.
> But thou betakest thee to the tavern before the town-gate,
> Each one ready with a bowl to blear both thine eyes,
> To proffer what thou shalt have, and what thy heart pleases,
> Wife, widow, or wench, that is wont there to dwell.
> Then is it but 'Fill in!' and 'Fetch forth!' and Florrie appears;
> 'We-he' and 'Whoa-up', words that suffice.
> But when this bliss is passed, the bill must be paid.
> Then must ye lay pledges, or your land ye must sell.*

For others, there was no escape:

> I saw a poor man near me hanging onto his plough:
> His coat was of a cloth that was called 'cary'
> His hood was full of holes and his hair stuck out,
> Through his worn shoes with their thick soles
> His toes peeped out as he trod the land:
> His stockings hung down his shins on every side,
> All dirtied with mud as he followed the plough.
> Two mittens he wore, made all of patches
> The fingers were worn through and covered with mud.
> The fellow wallowed in mud up to his ankles:
> Four heifers went in front of him, feeble and worn,
> You could count each rib, they were so sorry.
> His wife walked with him, with a long goad,
> In a short coat shortened again,
> Wrapped in a winnowing sheet to keep off the weather,
> Walking barefoot on bare ice till her feet bled.
> And at the field's end lay a little crumb-bowl,

* *Winner and Waster,* ed. & tr. Sir I. Gollancz, D. S. Brewer, Cambridge, 1974.

In it lay a little child covered in rags
And two more two year olds on the other side,
And all of them sang a song that was sad to hear
They all cried one cry – a mournful tune.
The poor man sighed deeply and said: Children, be quiet!*

It was little wonder that the other side of Richard II's reign, at the opposite pole to his glittering, international court, was the Peasants' Revolt of 1381, the most forceful of a series of disturbances in the later Middle Ages: when men asked in despair

When Adam dug and Eve span
Who was then the gentleman?**

---

* Piers the Plowman's Creed: author's translation based on H. S. Bennett, *From Chaucer to Caxton*. O.U.P. Oxford, 1926.
** See colour plate 4.

THE MERCHANT AND THE TOWNS

🔲🔲🔲🔲🔲🔲

IN the heart of the older towns of Britain there are often traces of the medieval town: narrow gates which are far too small for today's traffic or the remains of a ring of walls which might just be big enough to enclose the shopping centre. For medieval towns were far smaller than the huge sprawl of modern cities. In 1377, London had between thirty and forty thousand people – the size of a country town of today – and it was by far the largest town in the realm. York, Bristol, Coventry and Norwich together could just equal its population; and Norwich, which was an important and wealthy centre, had a little over five thousand inhabitants. Norwich Cathedral could have held almost half the population of the town.

To medieval men, a city was something marvellous and strange, a splendid place whose streets seemed to be 'paved with gold'. William Fitzstephen in the twelfth century wrote: 'Among the noble cities of the world that are celebrated by Fame, the City of London, seat of the monarchy of England, is one that spreads its fame wider, sends its wealth and wares further, and lifts its head higher than all others.' William Dunbar in the fifteenth century described it in verses which glow like a miniature from a medieval manuscript:

> London, thou art of towns the *A per se*
>   Sovereign of cities, seemliest in sight,
> Of high renown, riches and royalty;
>   Of lords and barons, and many a goodly knight,

Of most delectable lusty ladies bright;
　Of famous prelates, in habits clerical;
Of merchants full of substance and of might:
London, thou art the flower of Cities all.

Strong be thy wall that about thee stands;
　Wise be the people that within thee dwells
Fresh is thy river with his lusty strands
　Blithe be thy churches, well-sounding be thy bells;
Rich be thy merchants, in substance that excels . . .

In the country, it was almost impossible for a man to rise from being a serf or humble freeman, to a great estate. There, the order of life was fixed. But in the towns it was possible to make one's way in the world by enterprise and energy (see plate 12). If a serf ran away from his village and lived in a town for a year and a day as a citizen, he could become a freeman. Most of the townspeople were tradesmen of one kind or another, from the humble craftsmen who specialized in one simple kind of work (see plate 13) to the rich merchants who might deal in great quantities of goods of very different kinds. Each trade had its own organizations, the guilds or fraternities, which laid down the rules for its members, and tried to keep outsiders from entering their particular business (see plate 14). Until a man was a member of one of these organizations, he was a 'foreigner': in London this meant that he could only set up shop in a certain part of the city, and he was forbidden to work in the open air outside his shop, which was the usual way of advertising what one had for sale.

Above the guilds and fraternities was the council, which ruled the town or city; just as a lord held his land from the king, so these councils were given authority to order their own affairs by a royal charter. Such a privilege was not easily obtained. The first such charters, as opposed to the less formal arrangements which the Anglo-Saxon *burhs* or boroughs had enjoyed, date from the twelfth century. Richard I, anxious to raise money for the crusade, and John, equally short of cash, granted large numbers of charters, mostly to existing towns. Under the terms of the charters, a number of burgesses (the name for inhabitants of a

12. Tradesmen, craftsmen and artists: from top left, preparing colours, artist at easel, organist, blacksmith, potter, sculptor, innkeeper, surveyor, scribe, clockmaker (top right).
From a 15th century manuscript.

13. Dyers at work.

borough) were to be chosen as the aldermen or councillors. Although the charters were new, the words they used go back to Saxon times, and many of the privileges they contained were not new but simply confirmed old customs. The charter of Henry II to London in 1155 spells this out, saying that the Londoners are to have the privileges and customs which they enjoyed in Henry I's time.

Because towns have always changed and grown and been rebuilt by each generation, very little has survived from the Middle Ages. The townsmen were not great patrons of the arts, and the richly furnished houses of the merchants have all disappeared. The papers that survive are mostly concerned with the dry details of business, and only important figures like Richard Whittington (Dick Whittington of the nursery rhyme) come to life at all. Richard Whittington was probably the son of a knight,

14. The guildhall at Thaxted in Essex.

and he married a knight's daughter, so he would have been a person of some importance even outside London. He was a mercer, or dealer in cloth and other textiles, and he had valuable connections with the wool trade: in particular, he was head of the wool 'staple', the organization which handled all England's wool exports. He was four times Lord Mayor, and made very large loans to Henry IV and to Henry V: when he gave a banquet in honour of Henry V and Queen Katherine in 1421, he is said to have ended the entertainment by burning £60,000 worth of bills which he had paid on the king's behalf. Like many rich merchants, in an age when preachers often insisted that riches were evil, he made great gifts to charity: and since he had no children, he left all his fortune to charity. Prisons, hospitals, libraries and churches, even the Guildhall of London itself, all benefited from his good works.

At the other end of the scale, London was no place in which to be poor; its lively attractions were only for those with money, as the author of the fifteenth century poem 'London Lickpenny' tells us. He first describes how he went to the law courts at Westminster in search of justice, but 'for lack of money I may not succeed'. Then he wandered out through Westminster gate and across the fields into London:

> Then into Cheapside I went my way,
> Where I saw many people stand:
> One bade me come near and buy fine cloth of lawn,
> Paris thread, cotton and linen . . .
> Then I went forth by London Stone
> Along Candlewick Street;
> Drapers they called to me at once,
> Offering cheap cloth for me to buy.
> Then came there one and cried 'Hot sheep's feet!'
> 'Rushes fair and green,' another began to sell.
> Both fine cod and mackerel I saw there:
> But for lack of money I could not succeed.
>
> Then I walked on into Eastcheap.
> One cried ribs of beef, and many a pie.
> Pewter pots they clattered in a heap.
> There was harp, pipe and psaltery.
> 'Yea! by cock! Nay! by cock!' some began to cry;
> Some sang of Jenkin and Julian to get themselves mead,
> Full fain I would have had a minstrel sing;
> But for lack of money I could not succeed.
>
> Into Cornhill at once I went
> Where is much stolen stuff around.

I saw my own hood hanging there
That I had lost in Westminster among the crowd.
Then I stared at it and looked at it long,
I knew it as well as I did the Creed;
To buy my own hood back, that I thought was wrong:
But for lack of money I could not succeed. (See plate 15)

15.   Open air market stalls in the 15th century.

The writer ends by saying that he will go back to his ploughing in Kent, and never come near a town again.

Indeed, town life must have been strange and bewildering to a countryman. A man might be more free and life might be more varied in a town: but town life was also much more closely organized and hedged round with rules and regulations. There were laws about building, designed to stop the risk of fire in a timber-built city, which insisted that walls should be stone and roofs should be tiled, not thatched: for the Great Fire of 1666 was the last of a succession of such disasters in London, and other towns suffered in the same way.

Disease was another problem, and the city fathers did what they could to keep the town clean. Most houses – in London at least – had proper drainage, and there were public baths maintained by the city; and from about 1350 onwards water was brought in from streams and wells outside the city in pipes. Only the very rich had water on tap in their own houses, though an enterprising wax-chandler in the fifteenth century tapped the city water supply for his own use. He was discovered because this made the fountain in the nearby street run low; which shows how little water was available. But these public services, although very advanced for the time, were not enough to keep the city healthy. The Black Death of 1349 was only the most spectacular of a series of outbreaks of the plague which attacked the towns and cities for the next three centuries: and although in the Black Death even the tiniest village was not safe, in less severe outbreaks the country was always relatively free of infection, and the wealthier citizens would take refuge there. And if the problem of scavenging pigs rooting in piles of rubbish was a peculiarly medieval one – in 1365 a tanner was fined £100 for keeping pigs in the city – other hazards are still familiar: at Nottingham the smoke from the coal burnt by the citizens was so thick and foul that in 1265 Queen Eleanor sought better lodgings outside the town. Sometimes country air and country ways must have seemed preferable: and even in the twelfth century, Londoners took their ease at Clerkenwell, outside the city walls, or, if rich enough, hunting in the shires around the city.

🐚🐚🐚🐚🐚🐚

SCHOOLS AND UNIVERSITIES

🐚🐚🐚🐚🐚🐚

SCHOOLS

In the early Middle Ages, people who had been taught in a
school to read and write were few and far between. Many of the
nobles could not read, and there is a vivid portrait in *Piers
Plowman* of the parish priest who could not read:

16.   Schoolmaster and pupils, from a 15th century manuscript.

4. Adam delving, from a 12th century window at Canterbury Cathedral

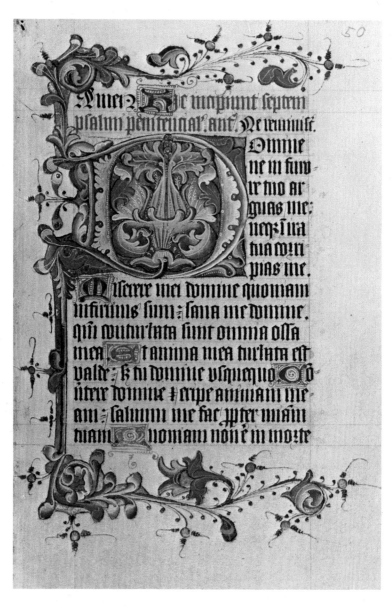

5. Decorated page: East Anglian work of about 1420–30

I have been a parish priest for more than thirty years, yet I can neither sing my notes right, nor read a lesson. I can start a hare in a ploughed field better than I can construe a single verse in the Psalms, or expound it to the parish.

There was no lack of schools, however, from the great church schools at cathedrals or monasteries (see plate 16), and the secular grammar schools in large towns (see plate 17), to the humble village school, often run by a parson who, unlike the one in *Piers Plowman*, had learned to read and write. Education was first and foremost for those who were to go into the church, at least until the fourteenth century. Henry I, nicknamed 'Beauclerc', the good scholar, was given a good education because he was the youngest of William I's sons and was expected to become a bishop: the historian William of Malmesbury tells how 'he received his first instruction in the beginnings of learning in a grammar school, and was so eager to drink in the honey of learning . . . that all the troubles of war and affairs of state failed to dislodge it from his noble mind'. Henry II, too, was known for his learning and love of books: both kings were regarded as exceptional by their contemporaries.

By the end of the Middle Ages it would have been exceptional to find a king who could not read, and most noblemen could also read and write. Merchants, too, needed these skills to carry on their trade, and men wishing to go to the universities required a special kind of learning. A variety of schools provided for their different needs. Nobles' and merchants' children, as well as future university students, all went first to a 'song' school, where they learnt to read and to sing the church services. They did not always learn much in the way of Latin grammar: in Chaucer's *Canterbury Tales* there is the story of the boy who could read and sing Latin psalms, but did not know what the psalm meant. They might also, if the teacher was skilled enough, learn to write, and to use Roman numerals for arithmetic. Instead of figures, letters represented different numbers: 8 was VIII and 10 was X. But if you tried to multiply you did not get very far – because 80 was LXXX! Multiplication and division were done on an abacus or set of counting beads.

17. The 12th century grammar school at Huntingdon.

If a boy went on to a grammar school, he would learn not languages, science or arithmetic, or even a craftsman's skill, but the lessons called the *trivium*. The *trivium* consisted of grammar, rhetoric (speaking) and logic (correct argument). These were not practical skills, but prepared the schoolboy for a professional career or for his university studies, and, at their best, taught him to think clearly and express himself clearly. William Fitzstephen, writing in the twelfth century, has left a vivid picture of London's grammar schools, both at work and play:

> In London the three principal churches . . . have famous schools by privilege and in virtue of their ancient dignity. But through the personal favour of some one or more of those learned men who are known and eminent in the study of philosophy, there are other schools licensed by special grace and permission. On holy days the masters of the schools assemble their scholars at the churches whose feast day it is. The scholars dispute, some in demonstrative rhetoric, others in dialectic . . . Some are exercised in disputation for the purpose of wit, which is but a wrestling bout of wit, but others that they may establish the truth for the sake of perfection . . . Boys of different schools strive one against another in verse or contend concerning the principles of the art of grammar or the rules governing the use of past or future. There are others who employ the old wit of the cross-roads in epigrams, rhymes and metre . . . they hurl abuse and gibes, they touch the weaknesses of their comrades, even perhaps of their elders . . .*

Just as books and letters were written in French and French was the usual language of the nobles, so teaching was done in French until the fourteenth century. John of Trevisa tells how the change came about:

> John Cornwall, a grammar-school master, changed the practice in grammar school, and the construing in French into English; and Richard Pencrych learned that manner of teaching from him, and other men from Pencrych, so that now, in 1385, in all the grammar schools of England children abandon French and construe and learn in English, and gain some advantage on one side and disadvantage on the other. The advantage is that they learn their grammar in less time than children used to; the disadvantage is that grammar school

* William Fitzstephen *Life of Thomas Becket* tr. H. E. Butler in F. M. Stenton, *Norman London*, Historical Association, London, 1937.

children know no more French than their left heel, and that is bad for them if they cross the sea and travel in strange lands.*

But as the grammar schools flourished, the old monastic and cathedral schools declined: in 1357, the Bishop of Exeter wrote of the schools in his part of England: .

> Among masters or teachers of boys and people who cannot read, who instruct them in grammar, a ridiculous and useless way of teaching is common . . . These masters, after their pupils have learned to read or repeat, even imperfectly, the Lord's Prayer, the Ave Maria, the Creed and other religious exercises, though they do not understand the words and what they mean, or how to use them, their masters make them go on to more advanced books of poetry. So they grow up without understanding things which they read or say every day . . .

Even at their best, these schools were never really designed to train schoolboys for entry to the universities. William of Wykeham, whose career in the royal service we have already looked at, founded a new kind of school at Winchester (where he was bishop) to fill this need. It was intended for those who, although rich enough to pay grammar school fees, could not get the kind of teaching from private tutors that they needed for the university. No scholar at Winchester was to have an income of more than five marks (£3·30) a year. This was as much as many parish priests earned, and much more than most craftsmen. Winchester was the forerunner of what we call 'public' schools today, but in some ways it was just as exclusive as they are now. Henry VI, in the middle of the fifteenth century, copied many features of Winchester when he founded Eton: but both Eton and Winchester remained exceptional schools. Indeed, the first scholars at Winchester profited so well from their education that they formed a distinct and powerful group in the government in the early fifteenth century.

* Quoted in A. F. Leach: *The Schools of Medieval England.* Methuen, London, 1915.

UNIVERSITIES

Most early medieval schools gave a general education only, and did not attempt to specialize. However, there were specialist professions for which further training was needed. In a very few places there were special schools which offered courses in these subjects, which were medicine, law and theology. In the eleventh and twelfth centuries, a man would have had to travel a long way to obtain teaching of this kind, and the few schools that existed had an international reputation. Adelard of Bath, tutor to Henry II and one of the most learned men in Europe in his day, travelled not merely to the schools at Laon and Tours, famous for their philosophy* teaching at that time, but also to Spain, Sicily, Italy and even to North Africa and Arab countries in search of learning. The oldest of all was the medical school at Salerno in Southern Italy. In the early twelfth century a great law school had developed at Bologna and at Paris the schools of theology were famous by the early twelfth century. The fame of a school often depended on an individual teacher. Peter Abelard is mainly remembered today for his autobiography, in which he tells of his tragic love-affair with Heloise. But he was famous as a great teacher. In the course of his career he taught at Paris and a number of other places. Even when he went into exile, in the depths of the country the students still 'gathered in crowds until there were too many for the place to hold or the land to support'.

From these schools at Paris and Bologna the first universities gradually developed. Teaching at Paris was controlled by the archbishop, and at Bologna by the city authorities. Gradually the teachers and students gained freedom from the control of outside bodies and formed their own organization. In Paris, the teachers decided who could become a teacher, while at Bologna this was in the hands of the students. Later universities followed the model of Paris. So it is fair to say that medieval universities were really teachers' associations. The church authorities still had some control, but this grew less as time went on. The course at

* Philosophy was a branch of theology, or religious studies.

Paris also formed the model for later universities. All students had to complete an 'arts' course, a training in speaking and arguing before they could go on to specialized subjects. These specialized or 'higher' subjects were medicine, law and theology, and anyone who held a degree in them received the title 'doctor', meaning a learned man.

Oxford was the first English university, and it was largely based on the model of Paris. Its cathedral schools were already famous in the twelfth century. When the author Gerald of Wales had completed his book about Ireland, he tells us himself that:

> he determined to read it before an audience at Oxford, where of all places in England the clergy were most strong and pre-eminent in learning. And since his book was divided into three parts, he gave three consecutive days to the reading, a part being read each day. On the first day he hospitably entertained the poor of the whole town whom he gathered together for the purpose; on the morrow he entertained all the doctors of the various faculties and those of their scholars who were best known and best spoken of; and on the third day he entertained the remainder of the scholars together with the knights of the town and a number of the citizens.

By the end of the twelfth century the schools at Oxford had become a university, the only one in England. But a rival, at Cambridge, developed when the students were temporarily banished from Oxford after riots between the students and townsmen in 1209. The constitution was similar to that of Oxford. In both universities, a college system was developed, under which the places at which the students lived also took care of their teaching (see plate 18). In this way they differed from European universities, where the students were divided according to their different 'nations'. Many English students continued to go to universities abroad, but by the end of the fourteenth century this was usually because they wanted to study a particular subject under a particular teacher.

University life was often violent, and the students had a bad reputation for drinking and fighting; battles between students and townspeople were common, and the students were un-

18. Master and scholars of New College, Oxford in the 15th century.

popular because they could usually claim the church's protection when they did anything wrong. Most students were in 'minor orders', that is, minor church officials. As such, they were not subject to the common law of the King, but to the much milder church law. Some of the trouble at least must have come from boredom and irritation at the length of the university courses (see plate 19). The basic arts course took six years before a student gained his master's degree. At Paris he was then required to teach for six years before beginning a theology course which lasted eight years. So by the time he was a doctor of theology, he had spent twenty years at university. Later this was made even longer, and forty was the usual age for qualifying.

19. A university lecture in the 14th century.

The universities did not really come into their own until the freer days of the sixteenth century. By then the Renaissance had made men less suspicious of new and daring ideas. But they had done much valuable work in preserving the tradition of learning which had been nourished through the Dark Ages by the monasteries. It is only because their greatest achievements were in theology and pure philosophy, both unfashionable today, that it is difficult to appreciate their most original work. After all, the university was the only place where a man thirsty for knowledge could quench his thirst. Richard Wych, Bishop of Chichester in the thirteenth century was one of these:

Such was his love of learning that he cared little for food or clothing. For, as he used to tell me, he and two companions who lived in the same room, had only their tunics, and one gown between them, and each had a miserable bed. So when one took the gown to go out to hear a lecture, the others sat in their room, and they used to take it in turns. Bread, with a little wine and soup, was food enough for them . . . yet he often told me how, in all his life, he never afterwards led such a pleasant and delightful existence again.*

Quite apart from the basic organization of the older universities, their rules and laws, much of their medieval appearance survives today. Both Oxford and Cambridge are rich in medieval buildings, still being used for their original purpose. The fourteenth century Old Court at Corpus Christi College, Cambridge, though much changed in detail, still houses undergraduates (see plate 20), while on a more monumental scale there are the chapels, gateways and even lecture-rooms such as the Oxford Divinity Schools, culminating in the glories of King's College Chapel, perhaps the greatest Gothic building in England. But King's College Chapel is a princely building; its magic transformation of stone into something airy and feather-light was brought about

20. The old court, Corpus Christi College, Cambridge: 14th century.

* G. G. Coulton: *Social Life in England from the Conquest to the Reformation.*
C.U.P. 1918.

by a king's riches, and must have astonished the 'poor scholars' by its magnificence.

Much more important than the buildings are the college and university libraries. Apart from a few later collections like the British Museum and the great American libraries such as the Pierpont Morgan Library in New York formed in the last hundred years, these hold almost all the medieval English manuscripts that have survived. At the Reformation in the sixteenth century the great monastery libraries were broken up, and the universities, always hungry for books in days when books were scarce, managed to acquire huge numbers of them. John Aubrey describes the fate of many manuscripts in the seventeenth century:

> I remember the rector here (at Malmesbury) . . . had several manuscripts of the Abbey. He was a proper man and a good fellow; and when he brewed a barrel of special ale, his use was to stop the bung-hole, under the clay, with a sheet of manuscript; he said nothing did it so well: which methought did grieve me then to see.

The manuscripts in college libraries were saved from this fate, and can still be seen there; nowadays they are locked in bookcases, and a few are on display, but even in the Middle Ages they were too precious to be left loose on the shelves. The old chained libraries survive at Merton College, Oxford and elsewhere, a reminder of the days when books could often only be read under the watchful eye of the librarian. Books were sometimes available for hire, but only the richer students or those working for their higher degree would have used these. The reason for the rarity and high price of books was that each was a manuscript, written by hand (see plate 21). The manuscripts which are most familiar to us now are the lovely illuminated masterpieces where scribe and artist have worked together, and which took several years to complete (see colour plate 5); but even the plain text of a manuscript took a very long while to write out when the tool was a quill pen and home-made ink, and the writing was done on parchment, a kind of specially prepared leather.

21. Eadwin the scribe at work: from a 12th century manuscript.

The world of the universities, and of learning and literature generally, was a very small one; it was only in the sixteenth century that men began to think of a university education as part of a general education rather than a kind of specialized training course; and to a large extent this change was made possible by the invention of printing, which made books much easier to produce. But even today the basic method of university teaching is still the 'lecture', a direct descendant of the medieval system of a master reading a text to his pupils and then commenting on it.

THE CHURCH

JUST as the church's need for men trained in its special learning determined most of what was taught at the universities, so the church played a very much greater part in every other part of life than it does today. For medieval men, the world of human society and the world of the church were the same, and could not be separated. The pope was recognized as head of the Christian world throughout western Europe, and no one seriously challenged his position.

But the church was not as strong as it might have seemed in theory. From the early Middle Ages, there was continual battle between the religious and royal organizations. They were both equally wide-ranging: the church had a priest in each parish, while the king had to rely on the local lord, who was often not very trustworthy. To complicate matters, the church was the greatest single owner of land in Britain; and since all land was officially held from the king in return for service in the king's army, this again led to disputes. A bishop was not just a lord of the church, he was also a baron, and a very powerful one too (see plate 22).

Though the conflict between king and church never became open war, as it did in Germany, the murder of Thomas Becket in 1170 by four of Henry II's knights was largely because of Becket's attempts to insist on what he thought were the church's rights (see plate 23). These involved a completely separate system of courts for clergy, which usually handed out much lighter sentences than the royal courts; and anyone in 'minor orders', such

22. An archbishop, drawn by Matthew Paris.

as a student or churchwarden could claim benefit of clergy, even though he was not actually a priest. The church also claimed rights such as that of sanctuary, whereby criminals could take refuge from the royal officers in certain churches. All of this was bound to cause problems when Henry II was trying to make justice the same for everyone and to enforce it more strictly. In the end, a compromise was reached: the church did not press its more extreme claims, and the king did not try to interfere in the church's own affairs.

The pope's authority was too distant to be a serious threat to the king in England. For much of the Middle Ages there were rival popes, each claiming to be the true ruler of Christendom, which meant that the church's political strength was weakened. Just the same, religion played an enormous part in medieval life. Almost everyone went to church on Sunday. Even though they did not understand the Latin words of the ceremony – and indeed the priest who said them had sometimes very little idea of what they meant – the great stone building and its marvellous paintings and carvings made a deep impression. The church was not only the largest building in most towns and villages: it was also the place where most of the important events of a man's personal life happened. Everyone was baptized, married and buried in a church. Churches were full of life, crowded with people: the problem was not how to fill them, but how the priest was to make himself heard above the hubbub of the congregation. For mass on Sundays was a social occasion, and the congregation took little direct part in the service (see plate 24). So it was hardly surprising that preachers had to warn women against gossiping and chattering during the most solemn parts of the service.

> Tutivillus, the devil of hell,
> He writes their names, truth to tell
> *Who chatter at the Mass.*

The bells rung at these high moments were once as much a call for silence as part of the ritual.

More medieval churches survive almost intact than any other kind of building of that time. Yet they are at best only shadows

23. The murder of Thomas Becket in 1170.

of their former selves, however glorious to the eye. They are
empty of people, except on the rarest occasions; and changing
ideas have led to the removal of the statues and paintings which
once made them blaze with colour. Sometimes this simplicity of
decoration has revealed the soaring brilliance of the architecture
better than ever before: but the life and warmth are all too often
missing.

What we see today are usually the churches of the later part
of the Middle Ages, when Britain was a relatively rich country,
and even small villages could raise a marvellous building in the
latest Gothic style 'to the glory of God'. But there are still some
traces of what went before, though Britain has nothing to compare with the smaller Romanesque – eleventh and twelfth century
– churches of France. The few churches of this period, called

24. Priest saying mass.

25. Doorway at Barfreston Church, Kent.

'Norman' in Britain, are usually fairly ample buildings, with massive pillars and rounded arches and little decoration. Occasionally, as at Kilpeck in Herefordshire or Barfreston in Kent, the work of some unknown genius survives (see plates 25 and 26). Barfreston echoes churches on the continent, and its balanced, formal style is a reminder that the classical tradition of Rome was still looked back to as the ideal for much of the Middle Ages, though there are not many echoes of it in architecture. Cathedrals were a different matter: in its day, Durham Cathedral, built at the end of the eleventh century, was one of the most advanced examples of architecture in the western world (see plate 27).

Architecture remained an international art throughout the Middle Ages: we shall see how masons and architects travelled from country to country. But one style is particularly English: we call it 'Perpendicular' because of its strong vertical lines, pillars rising unbroken to dazzling heights. It dates from the fourteenth and fifteenth centuries, and every county has its own superb example. Some of the most familiar images of England stem from it. Westminster Abbey is its forerunner, the spire of Salisbury Cathedral and King's College Chapel in Cambridge its chief marvels. Two areas in particular are rich in smaller churches in this style: the Cotswolds and East Anglia. Both were very wealthy parts of the country at this time, because wool, England's most valuable export, came from their pastures. Because they have never again been as rich, the churches have survived unchanged (see colour plate 6). Here the elaborate stone vaulted roofs are replaced by wooden roofs, particularly in East Anglia, where stone was difficult to come by: but the medieval carpenters could match any mason in contriving a richly decorated covering for God's house. But the great carved angels of Blythburgh or the intricate hammerbeams of Grundisburgh or Wetherden remind us of change as well as survival: the 'wool churches' remain, but the landscape is no longer a wide expanse dotted with sheep.

Occasionally chance, or remoteness from the great tides of fashion, have preserved things which were once common in churches. Medieval rood-screens, masterpieces of the wood-

26. Doorway at Kilpeck Church, Herefordshire.

carver's art, are very rare: they carried a carved scene of the 'rood' or crucifixion, and spanned the whole church. There are some fine examples in Norfolk and Devon. Wall and roof-paintings are rarer still (beware Victorian Gothic imitations, which are not medieval, though they may be lovely in their own right). For a view of the ordinary man's ideas of religion, turn first to the angels soaring above Blythburgh aisle; and then to the doom

27. Nave of Durham Cathedral.

painting, found under centuries of whitewash at the little church at Chaldon in Surrey (see plate 28). If the idea of heaven was not enough to fire a man's imagination, with its promise of release from toil and misery, then there was the threat of hell, which was a very real place in medieval belief, where earth's miseries would become tortures a hundred times worse. The angels and demons were not mere decoration. A preacher would point to these powerful images as he spoke, which, in an age when very few could read, formed a vivid part of people's beliefs about religion.

Preachers who could speak simply and directly to ordinary people were vital to the church. The ordinary parish priest, as we have seen, could often barely read; and his sermons were limited to the four which he had to give each year. So a special order of preachers, the friars, grew up in the thirteenth century. The two orders of friars, Dominicans or Black Friars and Franciscans or Grey Friars, were the missionaries of the church

28. Doom painting at Chaldon Church, Surrey: St Michael is weighing the souls in the centre against their sins. If their sins are heavier, they go to hell, on the left.

(see plate 29). They travelled up and down the country, living only on what they were given, preaching to ordinary people. That, at least, was the ideal which St Francis of Assisi, founder of the Franciscans, had set out to achieve, insisting that the brothers should own nothing. The friars, at best, provided a living example of holiness to ordinary folk. They also provided some of the great university teachers and thinkers of the four-teenth century. But they were beginning to stray from their original purpose. The picture of the friar that has come down to us in poems and stories of the time is very different from St Francis' simple brother. Chaucer thought there 'was little between a friar and a fiend', and an unknown writer contrasted their ideals with what really happened:

> Men may see by their countenance,
> That they are men of great penance,
> And also that their sustenance
> > Simple is and sparse.
> I have lived now forty years,
> And fatter men about the ears,
> I never saw yet than are these friars,
> > In countries where they roam.
> Meatless, so meagre are they made,
> > And penance so wears them down,
> That each one is a full horse-load
> When he rides out of town.*

Their begging was unpopular, too: they were accused of selling gifts and trinkets like ordinary pedlars, and of always being sure to call when a wife was alone at home, because she was easier to persuade than her husband.

Friars were more open to attack because men still thought of them as strangers and newcomers to Britain. Monks were often just as corrupt in their ways. But they were more respected, both because they had been here for many centuries, and because their power and good works were more in evidence (see plate 30).

* Song against the Friars, printed in H. S. Bennett, *From Chaucer to Caxton*: author's translation.

29. Franciscan Friar,
from a manuscript of 1427.

The abbots, rulers of the great monasteries, were the equals of bishops, and in the later Middle Ages sat in parliament: while the revenues of the monasteries, from sheep-farming in particular, were often very great. At best, the monasteries were places of prayer and study, whose work in caring for the poor and sick – who depended entirely on charity – and in preserving and spreading knowledge was invaluable. They also provided shelter for passing travellers, especially for pilgrims.

In the twelfth century, the greatest English monasteries were St Albans, St Augustine's at Canterbury and Bury St Edmunds. Of these, St Augustine's was the largest in members, with over a hundred monks: there would have been four or five times that number of other men there, including lay brothers, servants, and novices who were not yet monks. It was not a particularly dis-

tinguished monastery: most of the latter half of the twelfth
century was spent in an argument over rights with the archbishop of Canterbury. On the other hand, St Albans, where
there were about half as many monks, was a great home of learning, and its chroniclers in the early thirteenth century have left
an invaluable history of the times. Matthew Paris, the greatest
of them, was also one of the earliest of British artists, and we
shall return to his work. At times the chronicles seem to be
written with inside knowledge of court affairs, and become a
kind of official history. St Albans was also well placed with the

30. Monks chanting, from a manuscript of about 1340.

pope in the 1150s, because the only Englishman ever to become pope, Hadrian IV (Nicolas Brakespeare) had been a monk there. Brakespeare's career led him first to the schools of Paris and then to a monastery in the South of France, where his reforming energy led to a court case at Rome. However, this led to a papal decision in his favour and a series of appointments on papal service. He worked for some years in Sweden and Norway with great success, reorganizing the church there, and was elected pope in 1154. His rule was brief, since he died in 1159.

In contrast to St Albans, Bury St Edmunds was a monastery rich in lands and largely interested in managing its estates, though it too produced marvellous illuminated manuscripts in a highly original style, with strange creatures peering from the margins. A chronicle written there by Jocelin of Brakelond in the early thirteenth century is not concerned with great affairs of state but with the everyday matters of monastery life. The central figure is Abbot Samson, a powerful and gifted personality. He had been to the schools of Paris, but he wore his learning lightly, and preferred an active life, dealing with the abbey's great business interests. He 'prosperously ruled the abbey entrusted to him for thirty years and freed it from a burden of debt, while he enriched it with privileges, liberties, possessions and spacious buildings.' Jocelin has left a lifelike portrait of him:

> Abbot Samson was below the average height, almost bald; his face was neither round nor oblong; his nose was prominent and his lips thick; his eyes were clear and his glance penetrating; his hearing was excellent; his eyebrows arched, and frequently shaved; and a little cold soon made him hoarse. On the day of his election he was forty-seven, and had been a monk for seventeen years. In his ruddy beard there were a few grey hairs, and still fewer in his black and curling hair. But in the course of the first fourteen years after his election all his hair became white as snow.
>
> He was an exceedingly temperate man; he possessed great energy and a strong constitution, and was fond both of riding and walking, until old age prevailed upon him and moderated his ardour in these respects.

He was an eloquent man, speaking both French and Latin, but rather careful of the good sense of that which he had to say than of the style of his words. He could read books written in English very well, and was wont to preach to the people in English, but in the dialect of Norfolk where he was born and bred. It was for this reason that he ordered a pulpit to be placed in the church, for the sake of those who heard him and for purposes of ornament.

The abbot further appeared to prefer the active to the contemplative life, and praised good officials more than good monks. He rarely commended anyone solely on account of his knowledge of letters, unless the man happened to have knowledge of secular affairs, and if he chanced to hear of any prelate who had given up his pastoral work and become a hermit, he did not praise him for this.*

The picture of Samson is all the more interesting because he was not an important national figure; yet in Brakelond's narrative he dominates everything, because local happenings were so much more immediate than the distant doings of king and court.

The church was by far the most complex of medieval organizations, and these brief glimpses reveal only a few of its many different aspects. Because it has changed so much, and yet has left behind so many monuments to another age, it is the most difficult part of medieval life to recapture. Even its soaring music, brilliant manuscripts and graceful buildings bring us hardly any nearer to its true heart, the great mass of people who really believed in its teaching. The church was everywhere in medieval life.

* Jocelin of Brakelond, *Chronicle*.

MEDICINE AND SCIENCE

ALTHOUGH much of the care of the sick was in the hands of the church, medieval clergy were suspicious of doctors. Their learning and skills came dangerously near to matters of life and death on which only the church could say what was right. And their training led them into other dangerous waters, those of observing and recording knowledge and forming their own opinions without referring to traditional knowledge. 'Where there are three doctors, there are two atheists.' In the early twelfth century we find an abbot of Abingdon, Faricius, who was skilled in medicine. He had trained at the great medical school at Salerno and was doctor to Henry I and Matilda. But in the thirteenth century monks were actually banned from practising medicine, and the profession became entirely secular.

Doctors were always few and far between. The course for a doctor of physic's degree took a long while, and the chief centres for medical studies were abroad, at Montpellier in southern France and Salerno in Italy. From these schools and their teaching all medieval English doctors took their ideas. Early medical manuals such as those of John of Gaddesden and John Arderne in the fourteenth century, borrowed extensively from Italian works; and John Arderne's instructions to the doctor on how to behave when visiting a patient go back to a writer at Salerno in about 1100 (see plate 31). Nonetheless, this was the accepted and correct teaching, and even the greatest doctors never questioned its value until the sixteenth century.

For most people, sickness or injury would be dealt with by the

funguf de nare
fic incidinur.

31. Twelfth century eye surgery.

barber-surgeon and by neighbours who were skilled in healing
and medicines, using remedies which had been handed down for
centuries. These remedies had either been discovered by chance,
or went back to the same learned tradition from which the doctors
of physic themselves drew their knowledge. Indeed, some of the
stranger folk remedies come from a misunderstanding of learned
ideas, while the more effective ones were based on simple experience. Some of the remedies depended on things we do not fully

understand today, such as the charming of warts. Wart-charmers can still be found among country people, and they can undoubtedly make warts disappear. Nowadays we find this mysterious. To medieval people it was natural and straightforward, because they believed in invisible powers which could be good or evil. The good spirits produced cures; evil spirits were behind witchcraft. Though witchcraft was generally believed in, the great age of witch-hunts and witch-burning was not the Middle Ages, but the sixteenth and seventeenth centuries.

All this may seem a long way from medicine; but medieval men did not think of their bodies as a complicated machine, but as something halfway between matter and spirit, open to all kinds of influences, not least those of the stars. Astrology, the study of the influence of the stars on human existence (see plate 32), was much more important than astronomy, the mapping out of the stars in the heavens. Nowadays astronomy reigns supreme and astrology has sunk to a kind of fortune-telling in the newspapers. But medieval scholars took it very seriously, and many treatises on it and its relation to medicine and even to politics appeared. It lingered on into the seventeenth century, when modern scientific methods discredited the ideas on which it was founded. Many other poetic notions perished with it, such as the idea that the planets and stars as they moved across the heavens each gave out a particular musical note, which made a lovely harmony, 'the music of the spheres'.

The universities, where we would nowadays expect to find the greatest scientific knowledge, only tolerated attempts at scientific thought reluctantly, and often actively persecuted the philosophers who tried it. Roger Bacon, one of the boldest thinkers at Oxford in the thirteenth century, had a very chequered career, which was not helped by his outspoken and aggressive writings. His experimental work merely earned him a reputation as a magician, and the same was true of Robert Grosseteste, Bishop of Lincoln, his master. Bacon was born about 1220, and went to Oxford at fourteen. In 1240 he went to Paris, returning about seven years later, intending to continue his theological studies. But instead he concentrated for ten years on experiments in

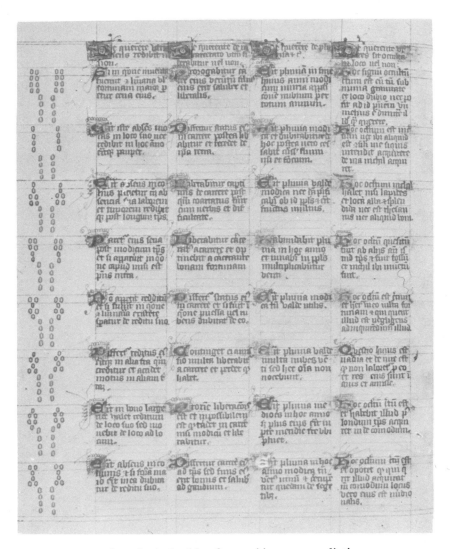

32. Astrological tables for working out predictions
from a late 14th century manuscript.

alchemy (chemistry) and optical science. In 1257, he became a
friar, a strange decision because it meant that it was more difficult
for him to study and write. Yet he continued his researches, and
wrote most of his books between 1257 and his death in 1292.
His work seems remote and curious to us today, because his
great interests were alchemy and astrology, and he claimed that

both were essential to mankind. Alchemy, the medieval equiva-
lent of chemistry, concentrated chiefly on the search for ways of
transforming one metal into another, in particular alchemists
searched for the 'elixir of life', a potion which would prolong
life, and the philosopher's stone, which would turn ordinary
metals into gold. Many of the most curious beliefs of the time
were involved. Bacon himself asked in all seriousness, quoting
such a belief as evidence, 'If deer, eagles and snakes can prolong

33.   An astrolabe, probably made in England about 1370.

Blythburgh Church,
Suffolk

7. St Paul at Malta:
wall painting in
Canterbury Cathedral
crypt

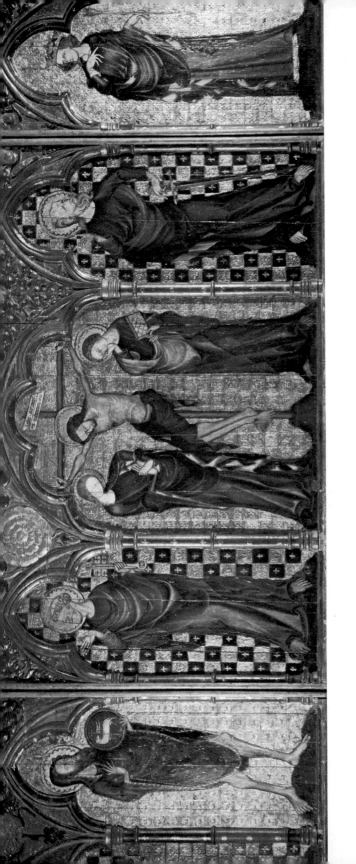

8. Altarpiece of Thornham Parva Church, Suffolk, 14th century

34. The clock at Wells Cathedral: 14th century.

their lives by using toads and stones, why should the discovery of an elixir of life be denied to men?'

On the other hand, the very fact that experiments and observations were made encouraged men to begin to work out practical uses for them. The astrolabe was used both in astrology and in navigation (see plate 33). Bacon's successors at Oxford tried to make accurate measuring instruments. They used their ideas about observation to write practical books on weather forecasting. William Merle based his little book on the subject on a weather diary which he kept from 1337 to 1344. The idea seems simple enough today: but medieval thinkers usually started with the theory and tried to apply it to real life, instead of working the other way round.

Matters of this kind had little effect on everyday life: science was still simply *scientia*, knowledge, rather than something practical. Yet there were new inventions and discoveries. The first windmills were built in the thirteenth century, and this meant that men who lived where there were no streams to work a watermill could grind their corn more efficiently (see plate 51). Improvements were made in the craftsman's tools: the first carpenter's bit and brace appears in the fifteenth century, the first spinning wheel in the thirteenth. And new, almost mass production, methods made iron much cheaper and easy to make. The first accurate mechanical clocks date from the fourteenth century: one of them survives at Wells Cathedral (see plate 34). Compasses, like clocks, were derived from Arabic books, and were known in England by 1300. Spectacles, brought from Italy, appeared in the fourteenth century. The most far-reaching invention of all, which was to change the whole pattern of war, was the arrival of gunpowder from the East by the early fourteenth century. Cannon were used for the first time in England perhaps in 1319 at the siege of Berwick, and were certainly available in 1327. The early cannon were almost as deadly to the people who fired them as to the enemy, and it was not until about 1450 that they became a serious threat to the old methods of waging war.

🔁🔁🔁🔁🔁

ARTISTS AND CRAFTSMEN

🔁🔁🔁🔁🔁

ARCHITECTS AND MASTER-MASONS

THE most spectacular achievements of medieval men were their great buildings, cathedrals and castles. Of Anglo-Saxon buildings, only Edward the Confessor's new abbey church at Westminster can begin to compare with the great Norman and English Gothic

35. Masonry at Winchester Cathedral, showing old and new methods: the old work is rough, made to fit with mortar, the new work, closely fitted, can be seen on the right.

cathedrals. Within fifty years of the arrival of the Normans, Winchester, Durham and Bury St Edmunds had all been started, planned on a scale new to England. Their patrons used international architects and craftsmen, who based their designs on work done in Normandy and France. They introduced new skills, such as the accurate cutting of large stones, which made such vast buildings possible. The small-stoned rough masonry of Anglo-Saxon times gave way to evenly-worked pieces of 'ashlar', where large pieces were bonded with narrow veins of mortar, making the buildings more solid and smoother in appearance (see plate 35). A writer looking at the new buildings at Old Sarum (Salisbury) in the early twelfth century said that the work was so closely fitted that it might have been made of a single rock. The Norman architects were daring, too: but their ambitions outran their skills, and as a result many of their more spectacular endeavours collapsed (see plate 36). The tower of Winchester, which fell in 1107 because of inadequate foundations, was the most dramatic of these episodes; but rebuilding started almost at once.

36.　Masons at work, from a 13th century manuscript.

The Normans built massively, using huge round pillars and thick walls; and later builders tried to refine their style, cutting away the masonry and introducing new forms such as the pointed arch and intricate windows with stone framing, until the later medieval buildings seemed like airy palaces of coloured glass. We know little about the early master-builders, even of such revolutionary buildings as Durham with its vaulted and ribbed stone ceiling. But by the fourteenth century individuals can be identified as responsible for a particular building. The most famous of English architects was Henry Yevele (see plate 37). He first appears as an important mason in London at the age of about thirty-five, in 1356, when he was chosen as one of the twelve master-masons who were to provide rules for their profession. Two years later he was working for the Black Prince at his house at Kennington, and in 1360 became the king's mason at Westminster Palace. This job meant that he also worked for the king elsewhere in the south of England. In the next thirty-five years he designed such varied things as a circular castle at Queenborough in Kent, the Abbot's House at Westminster, including the famous Jerusalem Chamber, a new chapel for the Black Prince at Canterbury Cathedral and the elaborate Gothic tomb of Blanche of Lancaster in old St Paul's. Much of Westminster Abbey is his design, as are the walls and windows of Westminster Hall, though the marvellous roof was designed by his fellow-craftsman, the carpenter Hugh Herland.

Like all medieval architects, Yevele was a practical builder as much as a designer. Nowadays architecture often needs complicated arithmetic to discover whether a design is possible. Yevele would have inherited such knowledge from the masters who taught him, mostly by word of mouth. Masons were famous for keeping their knowledge secret, and little of it was ever written down. Plans were usually worked out on the site: very few sketches of buildings survive in manuscripts, but one of the large plaster slabs on which the details of work to be done were drawn out survives at Wells Cathedral. We are used to seeing large buildings appear quickly, in a matter of weeks or months: medieval men, with very little power-driven machinery, had to work

37.   Roof-boss carving, said to be a portrait of Henry Yevele,
in the cloisters at Canterbury Cathedral.

slowly, and a cathedral could take tens or hundreds of years to
complete. Sometimes, as at Westminster Abbey, building work
would go on at intervals for a very long while. The foundations
of the present building date back to Saxon times: the central part
is of Henry III's period, from 1245 onwards; Yevele worked on

it in the fourteenth century; and the towers of the west end were only completed in 1740. (The most extraordinary example of this was at Cologne in Germany where the cathedral was started in 1248 and only finished six hundred years later.)

Yevele was also a master of carving and stone-working – the records call him a 'hewer' – and carved detail was always important in the great cathedrals. The Norman cathedrals tended to have only simple patterned decoration; but by Yevele's time every corner was filled with carving: weaving patterns of leaves, as at Southwell Minster, or an army of saints and stories from the Bible as on the font of Wells Cathedral. The ends and crossings of the ribs in the stonework, the ends of the stone gutters or the heads of pillars all had their face or flower or miniature scene (see plate 38), echoed on the seats of the wooden choir stalls in little carvings called misericords (see plate 39). For no labour was too difficult if it helped to make a church more beautiful and so proclaim the glory of God.

Yevele could also turn his hand to the very different problems of building castles. He carried out a number of military works,

38. Capital from Canterbury Cathedral, c. 1120: dragon killing a dog.

39. Misericord from Lincoln Cathedral, 14th century:
knight falling from his horse.

and may have worked on Bodiam Castle in Sussex (see plate 40).
Here he was working in a tradition which the Normans had
begun. The Anglo-Saxons built only very simple castles; mounds
defended by a fence and ditch. These were temporary, and not
meant for living in. As soon as the Normans had conquered
England, they began to build stone castles which were both
homes and fortresses. The earliest is the White Tower in

40. Bodiam Castle.

London, built by William I to control his capital city. It is four square in plan, and the early castles were all fairly simple. But in the twelfth century men coming back from the Crusades (see p. 117) brought new ideas. These were based on what they had seen in the East, while other ideas were developed at home. Henry II built an eight-sided castle at Orford, so that stones thrown at it from siege catapults were more likely to bounce off sideways (see plate 41). But the most spectacular of English castles were those built by Edward I's army engineers in Wales. These were the bases from which the English held down the

41. Orford Castle.

newly conquered Welsh princes. Because a large number of troops might have to live in them, they were very large. There is as much difference between these huge buildings and an ordinary castle with just a mound and a strong fence round it as there is between a cathedral and a parish church. We are so used to huge buildings nowadays that it is easy to forget how great an achievement they represent. Only those in a spectacular position like

42. Conway Castle.

43. Caernarvon Castle.

Conway or Caernarvon, still seem as dramatic and menacing as they must have done when they were first built (see plates 42 and 43).

PAINTERS AND SCULPTORS

Painters and sculptors worked closely with the architects on great buildings, because there was far more colour and far more statues in a medieval church than we see today. Because the paintings were usually done in a kind of colour wash on plaster, they often got damp and crumbled away, or the paint flaked off; so that only a handful survive. Some of these were rediscovered only recently under a coating of whitewash, put on in the sixteenth or seventeenth century when the Puritans were waging war on all kinds of images; many pieces of sculpture also suffered at the same time, but sculpture was more difficult to destroy. We can only guess at the lost riches of English painting in this period. Surviving treasures such as the St Paul at Canterbury Cathedral (see colour plate 7), with its overtones of Eastern art, or the painted apse at Copford in Essex, give us some hint of what the most skilled twelfth century artists could achieve. At the other

44. The 'worker's Christ',
St Breage, Cornwall,
surrounded by the tools
of different trades.

extreme are paintings showing Christ surrounded by the tools of humble trades (see plate 44)*, and the Doom painting at Chaldon (see plate 28), which are local efforts at church art.

The contrast between these and the first surviving 'panel' paintings, done in oil paints on wood, from the fourteenth century, is very striking. The most exciting pieces are from the court of Richard II : the portrait of Richard on his throne (at Westminster Abbey), and the famous Wilton Diptych, where Richard is presented by his patron saints to the Virgin Mary (see colour plate 2). The Virgin, with her glorious choir of angels, is the first great image in English painting. The Diptych may have been the work of a foreign painter who had learnt his mastery of technique in a French studio, but it was certainly painted in England for an English king. On the other hand, there is some-

* This may be an attempt to show Christ with the 'instruments of the Passion', the tools used in the Crucifixion, rather than Christ as patron of tradesmen.

thing very individual about the portraits on the left and about the grouping of the angels round the Virgin, particularly the marvellous upturned face of the angel who kneels and worships at her feet, which suggests an English master at work, a little less formal in his approach than the European painters.

Another masterpiece which has survived is almost certainly English, the altarpiece at Thornham Parva church in Suffolk: a crucifixion watched by stately saints whose grief is suggested rather than clearly shown (see colour plate 8). Its style is that of an enlarged miniature from a manuscript, relying on careful poses rather than individual characters to make its effect: but this was how the medieval painter worked. In the words of Walter Oakeshott, medieval artists have no interest in painting a natural picture of the world.

> If they draw a tree or a beast or a fish, they do so either because it is an essential part of their pattern; or because it is part of the story – as the lion is essential to the story of David rescuing the lamb from the lion's jaws; or because it is a symbol, like the lion of St Mark or the eagle of St John. The artist painting after 1450 . . . might draw Icarus falling from heaven, but the ploughman would be working in the fields. Business as usual. It is as if later painters had to make their religious pictures convincingly realistic if they were to persuade anyone to believe in them.*

Today we look at pictures as the reflection of the natural world, or as an artist's way of expressing his own ideas. For medieval men, a picture was an elaborate message which tried to explain a religious theme, or to say something about a king and his court. At its simplest this takes us to the anonymous figures of saints who are distinguished only by their haloes, tucked away in the corner of a stained glass window or in the initial letters of a decorated psalter. Or it takes us to the roof of the Great Hospital at Norwich, resplendent with a row of black eagles on a gold background in honour of Richard II. But it also leads to the complicated, enchanted world of the greatest manuscript illuminators. It is a difficult world to enter, because we no longer carry

* Walter Oakeshott, *The Sequences of English Medieval Art*. London, 1950.

45/46. Anglo-Norman craftsmanship: a candlestick made for Serlo, Abbot of Gloucester (early 12th century), and an ivory carving of the Virgin and Child with the Three Kings (late 11th century).

the key with us, and the locks are rusty. We need to know the Bible thoroughly, and the saints' legends as well: we need to know that St Catherine is shown with a wheel, like a catherine wheel firework; to know that St Lawrence is shown with a grid-iron and so on.* But even images which were commonplace, such as St Peter carrying the keys of heaven are unfamiliar today and where they do survive it is usually in a different place, like St George and his dragon on inn signs. So we can only look and marvel at the richness of the images themselves, unless their jewelled surface invites us to explore the meaning hidden beneath.

We can trace an artistic tradition from late Anglo-Saxon times right through the Middle Ages. This can be seen in metalwork and carvings (see plates 45 and 46). But it is clearest in manuscripts because they have been carefully preserved. The great monasteries were in some ways isolated from outside changes, and their work continued without interruption. In the eleventh and early twelfth centuries Winchester dominated the scene; then St Albans produced a series of masterpieces; and in the thirteenth and fourteenth centuries East Anglian artists at Bury and elsewhere created their own very individual style. The books from Winchester, much admired in their time, seem the most remote today, forceful but simple in their drawing.

With Matthew Paris, the great master of St Albans, we are in a more familiar world, particularly as many of his drawings are illustrations to the real happenings which he recorded in his chronicles. Matthew was born about 1200, and spent most of his life at St Albans. His work as a historian came to the king's notice by 1247, because Henry III spoke to him at a great festival on October 13 of that year and asked him to record it, 'in case in the future the memory of it should be lost to men who come after us'. In the following ten years, he seems to have been in close contact with the court; and he also travelled to Norway on church business. Otherwise we know little about him, except that he died about 1259. But he had left us one of the earliest self-portraits in English art, below his powerful image of the Virgin and Child at the beginning of his *History of the English* (see plate 47). The most famous of his 'natural' illustrations is that of the elephant presented by St Louis of France to Henry III, which Matthew

* In many cases the symbols were the instruments of torture by which the saint in question was put to death.

47. Virgin and Child, with self-portrait of Matthew Paris.

9 & 10. Two pages from the Douce Apocalypse,
illustrating St John's visions in the Book of Revelations:
above, the vintage of the earth, angels harvesting grapes;
below, the angel sounds the second trumpet

faciem tuam et sal
ui erimus · Exultate deo adiuto
ri nostro : iubilate dō
iacob. Sumite psal

11. Musician
initial in the early
14th century Bromholm
Psalter from Norfolk

12. A 12th century ship:
illustration of the whale
from a 12th century
book of beasts

also described in the text: but having put down a few words
about what it looked like he at once turns to his reference books
to find out how an elephant ought to behave, and copies that out
instead of continuing his own observations (see plate 48). He is
reluctant to wander far from accepted teaching: and even when
he does break new ground with his historical drawings, he tries
to invent his own set of symbols at the same time: the margins
are full of little symbolic sketches, such as a bell upside down
for the interdict (the pope's ban on all church services) during
King John's reign, when the bells were silenced (see plate 49).

The great manuscripts from East Anglia in the following
century are even more divided between the real and unreal
worlds. The Luttrell psalter offers on the one hand realistic
scenes of farming life and the changing seasons, as well as
domestic details like the cooking of a feast (see plate 50): on the
other hand strange grotesque creatures, half man, half beast,
emerge from the leaves and flowers in its borders. Similar

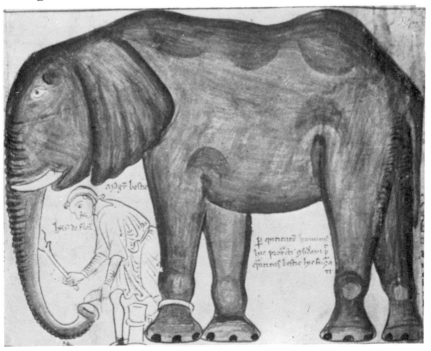

48. Elephant given to Henry III by St Louis of France in 1223.

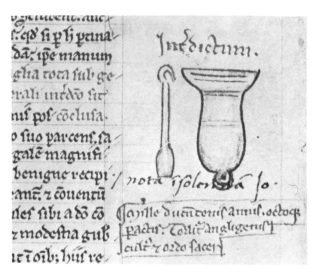

49. Bell upside down, symbolizing the silenced bells during the pope's interdict on England in King John's reign.

beings appear in other East Anglian works like the Ormesby psalter, as though the restrained, severe set-pieces of saints and crucifixions had been too much for the artist, and he had had to let his imagination run riot somewhere else. In the same vein are the little drawings of animals and scenes, sometimes satirical, sometimes coarse, but quite unconnected with the text (see plate 51). Here the distance between us and the unknown men who created these marvellous works seems greatest. Even if we share the same religion, we can only wonder at the

50. Cooking a feast, from the 14th century Luttrell psalter.

in confilio impiorum: & in uia pec
catorum non ftetit: & in cathedra pe
ftilentie non fedit.
Sed in lege domini uoluntas eius:
& in lege eius meditabit dieacnocte.
Et erit tanquam lignum qd plan
tatum est fecus decurfus aquaru:

51. First page of the Windmill psalter, 13th century:
note the windmill at the top of the page, and the monster in the border.

imaginative richness of extraordinary images like those in the pages of the Douce Apocalypse, an illustrated manuscript of the last book of the Bible, the Revelation (or Vision) of St John (see colour plates 9 and 10).

Sculpture, on the other hand, speaks more directly to us, particularly in the great portrait effigies from the tombs of medieval kings. Until the late fourteenth century, these splendid images of ideal rulers made no attempt to show what they looked like in real life, but offered the artist's idea of what they should have looked like. The Black Prince and Edward III appear, disguised as saints, in the Wilton Diptych: but there is far more character there than in their effigies. Only after Richard II's day, when he ordered that the tomb statues of himself and Anne of Bohemia should 'counterfeit' or actually represent them, do the real faces begin to appear. But then this brings us back to the great difference between medieval and modern art which we have already underlined. The medieval artist sees a king or a knight as someone who represents a certain rank, a fixed place in society, and shows him accordingly. He does not see him as an individual whose character may have little to do with his title. Contrast the effigy of the Black Prince (see plate 52), a formal, splendid hero, who might be Knighthood itself, with the real person shown in the portrait of Edward Grimston by a Flemish artist painted at

52. Effigy of the Black Prince in Canterbury Cathedral.

the very end of the Middle Ages (see plate 53). The age of the individual was about to begin.

53. Edward Grimston by Petrus Christus:
a portrait of a rich merchant of the 15th century.

POETS AND MUSICIANS

For three hundred years after the Norman conquest, the official languages in Britain were French (as spoken by the Normans) and Latin. Anglo-Saxon, which had produced great masterpieces of its own, became the language of ordinary people; and a writer who wanted to reach a wide audience had to use either French or Latin. Latin was a universal language – at least when it was written. When an international lawsuit between two Spanish kings was heard by Henry II in 1176 the proceedings had to be written out, because the English could not understand Latin as spoken by Spaniards. Official records and most important learned works were written in Latin, because it was the language used in schools, universities, and the Church. Even today the Roman Catholic church services can occasionally be heard in Latin, and some university ceremonies still use Latin. Books in Latin could be read anywhere in Europe without being translated; but only a small number of people in each country would understand them, a number which grew smaller and smaller as the years went by.

From this variety of languages English began to evolve as the common language of both nobles and ordinary people, but it was a gradual process. In the twelfth century, Geoffrey of Monmouth's 'historical novel' about the early kings of Britain and about King Arthur appeared first in Latin; then a French writer made a poem from it; and a Saxon priest from Worcestershire turned it into English. Geoffrey started with half-remembered Welsh stories, and added touches from recent history and from travellers' tales from the East. Wace, the French poet, put in details from his own knowledge of England, and Layamon the Englishman wove in images from the Anglo-Saxon world. The result was much richer and more varied than if only one writer had worked on it; and the same was true of the English language itself when it at last became the common tongue. Just as almost all the words in the French language can be traced back to Latin, so most words in Anglo-Saxon came from the German languages. So medieval and modern English very often have two words which mean almost the same thing, one Latin, one Germanic: we can say 'often' or 'frequently', and although the idea is the same, the words have a different feel. If we want to be pompous and formal, we use long Latin words; if we want to say something simply, we use Germanic words.

Medieval English had another source of richness which we have almost lost today, a host of dialect words. By and large, English today is the dialect used in the South Midlands in the Middle Ages; but when Caxton came to print the first English books in the 1470s, he was puzzled by these dialect differences. Eggs were 'egges' in some places, but elsewhere they were called 'eyren'; what was he to do? For medieval English was a spoken language, and its poets were still the close descendants of the minstrels and gleemen who recited their poems (see plate 54). Even in a very literary court like that of Richard II, Chaucer still read his poems in public. Only a very few people could afford to buy manuscripts for private reading, particularly if they were only romances for entertainment and not works for serious study. So most poems or romances were written for a particular audience, a lord's household or the royal court. Plays were mostly religious in nature, and were performed at great church festivals.

Many of the greatest works in medieval English are by unknown writers, and only in a few instances do we know much

54. Minstrels: from an
11th century manuscript.

about medieval authors. Where we do learn something of the personality behind the poetry it is either because they themselves have told us in their work, or because they were highly placed at court. Writers always earned their living in some other way: Chaucer was a civil servant, Langland, whose *Piers Plowman* shows the failings of medieval man, a poor clergyman. One of the most important medieval writers, the author of the Arthurian poem *Sir Gawain and the Green Knight* and of three religious poems, 'Patience', 'Pearl' and 'Cleanness', is completely unknown to us as a person. A poem quickly became separated from its author if it was passed on by being recited; and even if it was copied the scribes did not always add the author's name.

Medieval English writers worked in very different forms: there were no non-religious plays and no novels. Much of what medieval writers had to say was told as an allegory, where meanings have to be looked for. This, and the difficulty of reading a language often very different from our own, makes their writing something that we have to try hard to understand. But when we can understand, perhaps with the help of a modern version, there is a freshness about medieval writing that no other period can quite match, a feeling that language is something new and exciting. Just as painters began to see that they could recreate the real world in their art, so Chaucer's delight in drawing the rich characters of his Canterbury pilgrims is partly excitement at finding that literature can describe real people just as well as heroes or saints. There is the same freshness in the early poetry about the seasons; we are still close to the roots of things:

> Summer is a-coming in –
>   Loud sing, cuckoo!
> Grows the seed, blooms the field
> And green's the wood now.
>   Sing, cuckoo!
> Ewes bleat for their lambs
> Cows low for their calves
> Bullocks frolic, stags make wind
> Merry sing, cuckoo!

Cuckoo, cuckoo –
You sing well, cuckoo
Do not ever stop now.

Music and poetry were still closely connected: 'Summer is a-coming in' is also one of the most famous of medieval tunes. Most of the earliest surviving songs are religious (there is a religious text which fits the same tune as 'Summer is a-coming in') and one of the loveliest of these is St Godric's hymn to the Virgin Mary. Most such songs are by unknown writers, and are a mixture of plainsong, the church music of the time, with fashionable court songs such as those of the French troubadours. Even the fifteenth century Agincourt carol 'Our king went forth to Normandy' is a simple tune in the same general style. But behind the surface simplicity is considerable musical technique (see colour plate 11). 'Summer is a-coming in' is carefully arranged for six voices, and the Agincourt carol is also very much the work of a composer, working in a direct style.

More complex music was indeed being written in England by the end of the Middle Ages. Foreign musicians had led the way, and even in the twelfth century John of Salisbury complained of the excessive elaboration of the church music. In the fourteenth century John Wycliffe repeated this attack:

Then were Our Lady's matins [a church service] arranged by sinful men, to be sung with high crying to stop men understanding the meaning of what was sung, and to make men weary and not ready to study God's law because their heads ached; and in a short time more vain tricks were found – descant, harmony, organs and elaborate music, which make foolish men want to dance rather than weep . . . When there are forty or fifty in a choir, three or four proud and pleasure-seeking rascals will make the most devout service so elaborate that no one can hear the words, and the rest will be silent and look stupidly at them. And then they praise Jack the priest and Bob and William the proud churchmen: 'How finely they sing their notes,' and say that they serve God and Holy Church well!

So it is perhaps not surprising that it took English musicians a long while to establish an international reputation. Only in the fifteenth century, with John Dunstable, do we come to a really outstanding composer. Dunstable is a mysterious figure: we only know that he was already famous in Europe ten years before his death in 1453. His music, however, survives in European manuscripts; and his settings of the two Latin hymns 'Ave maris stella' and 'Veni creator spiritus' are a perfect match in their soaring beauty and daring structure for the achievements of the English churchbuilders of the same period. This music speaks more directly to us today than anything else from the Middle Ages: no translation or explanation is needed for us to enjoy its calm loveliness.

🈁🈁🈁🈁🈁

THE TRAVELLERS

🈁🈁🈁🈁🈁

MUSICIANS like Dunstable, writers like Chaucer, even monks like Matthew Paris, were travellers; but they were exceptional people. Ordinary men did not travel very much, and many did not even go outside the village where they were born. But others did nothing except travel. These were the merchants and pedlars, royal and church officials. Travel was far from easy, even if the journey was only across a county; and if it was abroad, there were all kinds of dangers and difficulties. St Godric, before he became a hermit (and musician) was first a 'chapman' by trade, a man who bought small objects like pins and knives from merchants in the towns and travelled round the countryside on foot selling them; but 'within a brief space of time, the youth who had trudged for many weary hours from village to village' became a merchant himself:

> He laboured not only as a merchant, but also as a shipman . . . to Denmark and Flanders and Scotland; in all these lands he found certain rare, and therefore more precious, wares, coveted by the inhabitants beyond the price of gold itself . . . Then he purchased the half of a merchant ship with certain of his partners in the trade; and again by his prudence he bought the fourth share in another ship. At length, by his skill in navigation, wherein he excelled all his fellows, he earned promotion to the post of steersman.*

After sixteen years as a merchant, he went on pilgrimage, to

* Quoted from translation of *Life of St Godric* in G. G. Coulton, *Social Life in England from the Conquest to the Reformation*, Cambridge, 1918.

55. Pilgrim, with scallop-shell badge and staff,
from a manuscript dated 1427.

Rome and to Compostela in Spain, travelling along the great
pilgrim roads like many hundreds of others who sought out these
shrines each year (see plate 55).

Godric would have voyaged or travelled without some of the
things which a later medieval traveller would have had: the
compass, first used in the thirteenth century, charts, or guides
for pilgrims. Though the charts were crude by comparison even
with seventeenth century maps, they were better than nothing

56. Map of England by Matthew Paris c. 1220–30.

(see plate 56). But the range of early medieval sailors was very limited by their vessels. In the twelfth century, even a Channel crossing from England to France was hazardous in the small ships of the time (see colour plate 12); witness the sinking of the White Ship in 1120, when Henry I's only son was drowned. St Godric did not venture beyond Denmark, Scotland or Holland. Even by the fifteenth century, little or no trade went by sea to the Mediterranean, though ships had begun to sail regularly to Portugal and to the Baltic Sea.

To the medieval mind, England was on the outer edge of the world, and therefore not a good starting point for exploration or voyages of discovery (see plate 57). The great medieval explorers set out by land for the East, and only one Englishman, Sir John Mandeville, ever claimed to have equalled the great journeys of the Italians. His book is really a kind of novel about the marvels of the East, and much of it is pure invention. But the book was a huge success and widely accepted as true. For a long while men had dreamt of a great Christian empire in the East, ruled by 'Prester John', who would one day come to the aid of western Christendom, overthrow the Moslems in Palestine and regain Jerusalem. Mandeville obligingly describes Prester John's empire, but he also offers good reasons why few people ever reach it:

> For in many places of the sea are great rocks of stones like magnets, that naturally draw iron towards themselves. And therefore there pass no ships that have either ties or nails of iron in them. And if any do come, at once the rocks like magnets draw them to themselves, and they can never go away again. I myself have seen afar in that sea, what looked like a great isle full of trees and bushes, full of many thorns and briars. And the shipmen told us, that all that was ships drawn there by the magnets because of the iron in them. And from the rotting ships there bushes and thorns and briars and green grass grew; and the masts and spars looked like a wood full of trees.

And he goes on to tell of more such wonders:

> For in his country is the sea that men call the gravelly sea, that is all

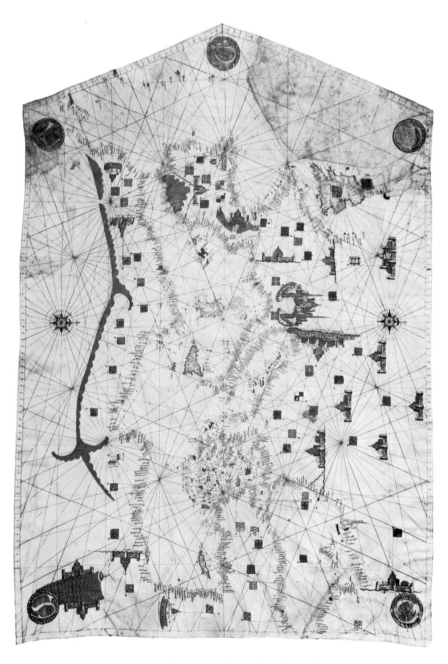

57. Portolan chart dated 1456.

58. Mappa Mundi, Hereford Cathedral, c. 1300.

gravel and sand, without a drop of water, and it ebbs and flows in great waves, like other seas, and it is never still. And no man may cross that sea in a ship or any kind of craft . . . Although it has no water in it, yet men find in it good fish of a different kind and shape than in any other sea, which are very tasty and delicious food.

Yet even here there are signs of a new way of looking at the world. The circle of the Roman and medieval *mappa mundi*, map of the world, was beginning to break (see plate 58). Men no longer really thought of an outer ocean around a land mass of which Jerusalem was the exact centre. Mandeville puts across the new ideas in his usual way, as a traveller's tale:

> I have heard told when I was young, how a worthy man once departed from our countries to go and explore the world. And so he passed India and the islands beyond India, where are more than five thousand islands. And he went so far by land and sea, and spent so many years travelling about the world that he found an island where he heard his own language spoken; a ploughman calling to his oxen and using the words that men spoke to beasts in his own country; and he was amazed, because he could not understand it. But I say that he had travelled for so long by land and sea that he had come right round the world.

But most English travellers made their weary way, on foot or on horseback, down the roughly repaired remains of one of England's old Roman roads. For them, as they kept a wary eye open for robbers and wondered whether they would manage the few miles to their destination before nightfall, Mandeville's ideas were 'travellers' tales' indeed.

㊉㊉㊉㊉㊉

THE KNIGHT AND WAR

㊉㊉㊉㊉㊉

FOR most of the Middle Ages, war rarely threatened England itself; yet it was a land organized for war. Every landowner held his land because he was able to serve in the king's army himself or to send someone in his place. The knight was the ideal of medieval men, and everywhere we find traces of this: in romances, carvings, and in politics and social life. The hero of the romance, the effigy on the tomb, the member of parliament, the man the merchant's daughter hoped to marry: all were knights. And a knight was by trade a soldier, even at the end of the Middle Ages (see plate 59).

But very few knights were professionals. Many of them had had some practice in arms, and would have fought in one or two campaigns, either against the Welsh, Scots or French. Others would simply have hired someone to go and fight in their place, or would have paid the king a fine, with which he would have hired someone. Occasionally, however, we find someone who was a really skilled fighter, and who made his fortune out of it. At the end of the twelfth century, William Marshal rose from being an ordinary knight's son to the earldom of Pembroke and acting ruler of England while Henry III was a boy. When William himself was a boy, King Stephen besieged the castle which his father held, and captured William. Stephen's men tried to get the garrison in the castle to surrender by threatening to hang William, but William's father made no attempt to save him and refused to give up even when a noose was put round his son's neck. Stephen took pity on the boy, and spared him. William grew up to be a very skilled horseman, and was tutor to Henry II's

59. Making a knight: drawing by Matthew Paris, early 13th century, showing him being given his sword, tunic and banner.

eldest son, Henry, even though he had little education himself and his fame was only as a fighter in tournaments.

Tournaments were a kind of mock war. In William's day, they were little different from the real thing, except that weapons were blunt and not sharp. There would often be a hundred or more knights on either side, and there were very few rules. Later, tournaments tended to be fights between individual knights, and the rules became very complicated. William needed all his strength and skill to do well in the early tournaments, particularly as anyone who was captured lost his horse and armour. As a younger son of a not very rich knight, William had to virtually beg horse and armour from another knight, and could not afford to lose it. In his first tournament, however, he did very well, capturing four knights. From then on he made a considerable amount of money out of his tournaments, by selling the captured equipment or by allowing captured knights to ransom themselves. Capturing a knight was not always that easy, even with a number of men on foot to help. At one tournament William's side chased their opponents right off the fields where the tournament was being held into a nearby town. Here William captured a French knight; but as they rode back out of the town through the narrow streets, the knight seized an overhanging drainpipe and swung himself out of the saddle. William did not notice, and arrived back with only the horse and saddle, much to everyone's amusement.

Affairs such as this were good training for hand-to-hand fighting in real war, and they occasionally did become a real war between enemies. On the other hand, they could be a useful outlet for knightly enthusiasts, as during the Hundred Years War, when tournaments were often arranged during periods when there was peace or even a temporary truce. By the fifteenth century, however, jousts (fights between two knights only) had replaced the earlier free-for-all, and were merely a kind of sport, part of any great festival such as a king's coronation or wedding, and they had little to do with real war (see plate 60).

60. Knights jousting, from a 13th century manuscript.

Even when it came to real war, the knights still regarded fighting as something of a sport. War was a little more dangerous, but it was usually the ordinary soldiers who suffered most casualties, while the knights, encased in armour, were rarely killed. In any case, the enemy did not try to kill them, but to capture them and ransom them, just as in tournaments. There is an incident from the Hundred Years War, when a Breton countess, ally of the English, was defending her castle with the help of English soldiers. The French had built a great machine with which to break down the castle walls, and the English went out one evening and destroyed it. As they returned to the castle, the enemy set out in pursuit of them. The leader of the English, Sir Walter

Manny, cried, 'May I never be embraced by my mistress and dear friend, if I enter the castle before I have unhorsed one of these gallopers.' A general skirmish followed 'in which many brilliant actions, captures and rescues might be seen'.

The great pitched battles which ended in dramatic victory or defeat – Hastings, Crécy, Bannockburn, Poitiers – were very unusual in medieval warfare. Most wars were long drawn-out affairs of sieges, skirmishes and ravaging of the countryside. War fell far harder on innocent farmers and labourers, on the men of small villages and towns, than on the soldiers or the great lords. The English were fortunate in that there was little fighting in England itself between the Norman conquest and the Wars of the Roses: and what there was, was mostly on the Scottish and Welsh borders. The Hundred Years War was fought out in France, and great areas were often turned into deserts for years on end after one army or another had passed through, just as William I's campaigns in the north of England had laid waste whole counties. War to the medieval Englishman was largely something strange and exciting that happened in distant foreign parts. An adventurous knight might have to travel to Palestine or to the eastern borders of Europe to find a war in which he could win fame.

Most of those distant expeditions were crusades of one kind or another. The 'crusade' or Holy War had originally been a campaign by the pope to win back Jerusalem from the Moslems who were threatening to bar the way to pilgrims from the west (see plate 61). The first crusade, in 1099, succeeded in capturing Jerusalem. But holding the newly-conquered city was more of a problem, and the new Kingdom in Palestine continued to need help from its fellow-Christians in the west. So the second, third, fourth and fifth crusades followed; and even in the fifteenth century, long after Jerusalem had fallen into Moslem hands again, men dreamt of a great expedition to win it back (see plate 62). Meanwhile, crusades had become a kind of general war against the heathen. They were being fought in eastern Europe as well, where the Teutonic Knights were conquering Prussia. The fourth crusade was not even directed against the heathen,

61. Christ leading the Crusaders, from a 13th century manuscript.

but against the Greek Christian empire in Constantinople. Crusades had become too political and complicated: the original ideal had been very simple.

The greatest of all English crusaders was Richard I, who, when he came to the throne, had already vowed to go to Palestine, and to attempt to recapture Jerusalem, which had been lost to the Moslems in 1187. Like many other crusaders, he was very enthusiastic about the idea of setting out to recapture Jerusalem. He took a vow to go on crusade in 1187, but he needed all his enthusiasm to see him through the delays that followed. Even when he managed to set out in 1190, the expedition was delayed on its way, first in Sicily, and again in Cyprus. But when he at last reached Acre, on the coast of Palestine, he was greeted joyously by the French troops who had already arrived and were

62. Kneeling crusader, drawn by Matthew Paris.

helping to besiege the city, which was in Moslem hands (see plate 63). One of Richard's companions described his arrival in almost poetic terms:

> No pen can sufficiently describe the joy of the people on the night of the king's arrival, nor tongue detail it; the very calmness of the night was thought to smile upon them with a purer air; the trumpets clanged, horns sounded, and the shrill intonations of the pipe, and the deeper notes of the tambourine and harp, struck upon the ear; soothing symphonies were heard like various voices blended in one; and there was not a man who did not, after his own fashion, indulge in joy and praise; either singing popular ballads to testify the gladness of his heart, or reciting the deeds of the ancients, stimulating by their example the spirit of the moderns. Some drank wine from costly cups to the health of the singers, while others mixing together, high and low, passed the night in constant dances. And their joy was heightened by King Richard's subjugation of the island of Cyprus, a place so useful and necessary to them, and one which would be of the utmost service to the army. As a further proof of the exultation of their hearts and to illumine the darkness of the night, wax torches and flaming lights sparkled in profusion, so that night seemed to be usurped by the brightness of day, and the Turks thought the whole valley was on fire.

Though Richard and his allies took Acre, and later inflicted several defeats on the Moslems, they were unable to attack Jerusalem. The nearest they came to it was to pitch camp a few miles away. One day Richard went out hunting from the camp, and came within sight of the Holy City: he is said to have turned away, to avoid seeing it, because he knew by then he could not capture it.

His opponent was the Moslem general, Saladin, who admired Richard's courage and generalship; when Richard fell ill, Saladin sent him presents of fruit and of snow from the Lebanese mountains to cool his fever, and when they met to negotiate a peace settlement, they talked on the friendliest of terms. This was in sharp contrast to the usual relationship between the crusaders and the Moslems, for there was a dark side to the high religious

63. Richard I, from a 13th century floortile from Chertsey Abbey.

zeal that kept the crusaders' spirits up in the most difficult moments. The crusade might be a holy expedition, but it was also a vicious war, and most Christian writers held that killing heathens, even in cold blood, was a virtuous deed. When the Christians took Jerusalem for the first time in 1099, they celebrated with a bloody massacre of the inhabitants. Even Richard executed the Moslems who had defended Acre when he took the city. The same mixture of cruelty and heroism is to be found in the Hundred Years War, with its great moments of chivalry contrasting with episodes such as the Black Prince's slaughter of the inhabitants of Limoges in 1370 when they refused to surrender to him.

But we must beware of thinking of medieval England in terms of these vivid contrasts only, whether we are talking about warfare or peacetime. Medieval chroniclers loved to highlight great events and make them even more dramatic than they really were; and medieval histories are largely written in highly coloured pictures, rather like the brilliant miniatures that decorate their pages. In real life there are great areas of grey between the splashes of vivid green or blue, and it is these grey areas are the ones that we have most difficulty in mapping out. The day to day routine of an army, the ordinary villager's life, the detailed business of government – all this forms a grey background to the coloured pageant we have looked at in this book.

🔳🔳🔳🔳🔳

CONCLUSION

🔳🔳🔳🔳🔳🔳

I HAVE already tried to suggest some of the physical links with the Middle Ages that survive today – buildings, manuscripts, works of art. The invisible links of thought and language are much harder to trace, but are just as real. In England, many of our institutions go back to medieval origins – parliament, itself medieval, is full of such reminders. The Chancellor of the Exchequer owes his name to the royal treasury where money was counted out on a 'chequered' cloth: the Privy Seal was the king's private seal; the parliament building itself still follows the layout of a medieval chapel, with rows of seats facing each other. (This alone has had a great effect on British politics – parliament naturally divides into two parties, which would not be the case if the building was laid out on a circular plan, as in France.) In English-speaking law courts, some laws handed down from medieval England still survive, and the idea of a jury is something which we owe to our medieval ancestors. Until a few years ago, British currency was medieval: and the 'pound' is a reminder of the days when it was a pound's weight of silver pennies. We still measure in medieval versions of Roman units; and many of England's roads still follow medieval pathways between towns and villages whose names were fixed in medieval times. For we have inherited much from the days when England was 'a strong land and a sturdy, and the most plentiful corner of the world, so rich a land that it scarcely needs help of any land, and every other land needs help of England. England is full of mirth and of game, and men often able to mirth and game, free men of heart and with tongue . . .'

◙◙◙◙◙◙

BIBLIOGRAPHY

◙◙◙◙◙◙

I. SOURCE MATERIAL IN TRANSLATION

Chaucer, Geoffrey. Trans. Cawley, A. C. *The Canterbury Tales*. Dutton, New York

Froissart, John. *Chronicles of England, France and Spain*. Dutton, New York, 1961

Malory, Sir Thomas. Ed. Cowen, J. *Morte D'Arthur*. (Vol. I and II), Everyman, Dutton, New York

Ed. Sisam and Sisam. *Oxford Book of Medieval English Verse*. Oxford University Press, New York, 1970

Trans. Stone, Brian. *Sir Gawain and the Green Knight*. Penguin, Baltimore

2. NON-FICTION FOR THE SAME AGE GROUP

Fraser, Antonia. *King Arthur and the Knights of the Round Table*. Alfred A. Knopf, New York, 1971

Fraser, Antonia. *Robin Hood*. Alfred A. Knopf, New York, 1972

Macaulay, David. *Cathedral: The Story of Its Construction*. Houghton Mifflin, Boston, 1973

Uden, Grant. *A Dictionary of Chivalry*. T. Y. Crowell, New York, 1969

3. FICTION FOR THE SAME AGE GROUP

Bibby, Violet. *The Mirrored Shield*. Longman Young Books, London, 1970

Bibby, Violet. *The Wilding*. Longman Young Books, London, 1971

'Bryher'. *The Fourteenth of October*. Pantheon, New York, 1951

Duggan, Alfred. *Leopards and Lilies*. Chatto, Landmark Library, London, 1971

Hamley, Dennis. *Pageants of Despair*. S. G. Phillips, New York, 1974

Harnett, Cynthia. *A Load of Unicorn*. Methuen, London, 1959. Penguin, Puffin Books, Harmondsworth, 1966

Harnett, Cynthia. *The Wool-Pack*. Methuen, London, 1951. Penguin, Puffin Books, Harmondsworth

Holland, Kevin Crossley. *King Horn*. Macmillan, London, 1965

Lewis, Hilda. *Gentle Falcon*. Oxford University Press, Oxford Children's Library, Oxford, 1966

Lewis, Hilda. *Here Comes Harry*. Oxford University Press, Oxford, 1960

Mott, Michael. *The Blind Cross*. Delacorte, New York, 1970

Picard, Barbara Leonie. *One Is One*. Holt, Rinehart and Winston, New York, 1966

Picard, Barbara Leonie. *Ransom For A Knight*. Henry Z. Walck, New York, 1956

Seton, Anya. *Katherine*. Houghton Mifflin, Boston, 1954. Fawcett World, New York, 1973

Shakespeare, William. *Richard II, Henry IV* parts I and II

Sutcliff, Rosemary. *Knight's Fee*. Henry Z. Walck, New York, 1960

Sutcliff, Rosemary. *The Witch's Brat*. Henry Z. Walck, New York, 1970

Tey, Josephine. *Daughter of Time*. Franklin Watts, New York. Berkley Publishing Co., New York, 1970

Treece, Henry. *The Children's Crusade*. Bodley Head, London, 1971. Penguin, Puffin Books, Harmondsworth, 1970

Treece, Henry. *The Golden One*. Bodley Head, London, 1961

Willard, Barbara. *The Lark and the Laurel*. Harcourt Brace Jovanovich, New York, 1970

Williams, Ursula Moray. *Noble Hawks*. Hamish Hamilton, London, 1965

4. WIDER READING

Brewer, D. S. *Chaucer In His Time*. Longman, New York, 1973

Coulton, G. G. *Medieval Panorama : The English Scene from Conquest to Reformation*. W. W. Norton, New York, 1974

Coulton, G. G. *Life in the Middle Ages*. Cambridge University Press, Cambridge, 1928

Evans, Joan, Ed. *The Flowering of the Middle Ages*. McGraw-Hill, New York, 1966

A. L. Poole, Ed. *Medieval England*. Oxford University Press, New York, 1958

Runciman, Sir Steven. *A History of the Crusades*. (3 Vol.) Cambridge University Press, New York

Trevelyan, G. M. *English Social History* I. David McKay, New York, 1965

5. RECORDS

Music of John Dunstable and his Contemporaries TV34058S

Music of the Middle Ages and Renaissance Vol I HQS 1195

Medieval English Lyrics ZRG 5443

England Be Glad! Patriotic and Heroic Songs and Music from the Crusades to the Civil War CFP 40015

Fifteenth Century Music SAWT 9505

Thirteenth Century Music SAWT 9530

𝕤𝕤𝕤𝕤𝕤𝕤

INDEX

𝕤𝕤𝕤𝕤𝕤𝕤